SpringerBriefs in Law

More information about this series at http://www.springer.com/series/10164

Lutz-Christian Wolff · Jenny Chan

Flipped Classrooms for Legal Education

Springer

Lutz-Christian Wolff
Faculty of Law
The Chinese University of Hong Kong
Hong Kong
Hong Kong

Jenny Chan
Faculty of Law
The Chinese University of Hong Kong
Hong Kong
Hong Kong

ISSN 2192-855X ISSN 2192-8568 (electronic)
SpringerBriefs in Law
ISBN 978-981-10-0478-0 ISBN 978-981-10-0479-7 (eBook)
DOI 10.1007/978-981-10-0479-7

Library of Congress Control Number: 2016931326

Printed on acid-free paper

This Springer imprint is published by SpringerNature
The registered company is Springer Science+Business Media Singapore Pte Ltd.

Preface

Flipped Classrooms have become a widely discussed topic in recent times. And, this is true also in the context of legal education. However, there is no standardized understanding of the notion of Flipped Classrooms and astonishingly little literature is available, not to speak about reliable data, confirming the viability of this new teaching method. The goal of this book is to conduct—on the basis of a comprehensive literature review—a detailed analysis of the Flipped Classroom concept in terms of pedagogical, technical and financial viability in legal education.

This book is based on the outcomes of the study project 'Flipped Classrooms for Legal Education in Hong Kong', which was conducted from March 2014 to February 2015. The Principal Supervisor of the study project was Lutz-Christian Wolff, Wei Lun Professor of Law and Dean of the Graduate School of The Chinese University of Hong Kong (CUHK). The driving force behind the project was Research Assistant, Mrs. Jenny Chan, then a part-time LLM student at the CUHK Faculty of Law and currently full-time research assistant at CUHK. Co-supervisors were Professional Consultant Elsa Kelly, Associate Professor of Practice Steve Gallagher and Associate Professor Michael Lower all members of the CUHK Faculty of Law. The authors are most grateful for the valuable input of the co-supervisors.

The study project was funded by a Teaching Development Grant of The Chinese University of Hong Kong (CUHK). We are thankful for the support granted by CUHK which has allowed us to conduct this interesting and important study.

Hong Kong
September 2015

Lutz-Christian Wolff
Jenny Chan

Contents

Chapter 1
Introduction

1.1 General

The book aims to analyze the feasibility of using Flipped Classrooms for this purpose of legal education. There are a number of reasons why this is an important topic as set out in the following sections.

1.2 Why This Topic?

1.2.1 Law Schools Today

The twenty-first century poses multidimensional challenges to legal educators around the world. In the U.K., the recent trend to decentralize educational powers has wheeled an increasing need for innovation in classrooms.[1] The Dearing Report was prepared in an attempt to overhaul higher education in the U.K. made 93 recommendations. One recommendation explicitly proposes that higher education should make greater use of technology and each student should have access to a portable computer.[2]

In the U.S., in an effort to address the inadequacy in how law schools are '*Educating Lawyers*', the Carnegie Foundation released a report, commonly known as the Carnegie Report.[3] The Carnegie Report concludes that today's law school curricula fail to address the needs of law students properly and makes five observations and seven recommendations regarding legal education.[4] It also openly

[1]Wallace, p. 293.

[2]See National Committee of Inquiry into Higher Education, the Dearing Report Recommendations No. 21, 44 and 46 for recommendation of greater use of technology.

[3]For details see infra, 3.4.5.2.

[4]The Carnegie Report Summary.

L.-C. Wolff and J. Chan, *Flipped Classrooms for Legal Education*,
SpringerBriefs in Law, DOI 10.1007/978-981-10-0479-7_1

criticizes legal education for its lack of professional training and the resulting inability of law students to discharge professional duties that lie ahead.[5] The Carnegie Report also explains deficiencies of the Socratic Method, the traditional teaching method in American law schools.[6] These deficiencies are discussed in more detail below.[7]

In Australia it has been observed that law schools, in addition to challenges arising out of resource constraints[8] and an increasing number of students,[9] have to address the fact that more students are nowadays engaging in part-time work.[10] These students find it difficult to attend classes and there seems to be a need for greater flexibility in the course delivery.[11] As discussed below,[12] one of the major arguments in favor of Flipped Classrooms is the perceived learning flexibility.

1.2.2 Modernizing Legal Education

In the modern world which often defines law schools by ranking competition,[13] law schools are market-driven.[14] Law schools need to distinguish themselves and one way of doing this is to adopt innovative teaching methods in order to produce out-performing students with better career prospects.[15] There is consequently an ongoing debate about if and how legal education should be reformed and technology seems to be one of the driving forces in this regard. The use of technology is one of the major features of the Flipped Classroom concept which is consequently in line with recent trends in legal education.

Despite these observations and the notable fact that there have been attempts to use new technology in legal education, anecdotal evidence suggests that law schools seem rather slow in embracing technology when compared with other disciplines.[16]

One explanation for a general disinterest in using new technology for teaching purposes in higher education and in particular in legal education might be that there is a genuine shortage of resources.[17] At the same time the developed world has

---

[5]Compare The Carnegie Report, pp. 23–24.
[6]*Ibid*, pp. 56–59.
[7]Compare *infra*, 3.4.
[8]Hewitt, p. 96.
[9]*Ibid.*
[10]*Ibid.*
[11]*Ibid*, pp. 96–97.
[12]*Infra*, 3.3.2.
[13]Henderson, p. 467.
[14]Compare Berger, p. 498.
[15]Compare Henderson, p. 501.
[16]Bone, p. 242.
[17]Catley, p. 2; Binford, p. 172.

faced a period of rapid growth in recent decades with an increasing demand for higher education as the Dearing Report had concluded as early as in 1997.[18] Statistics by Higher Education Statistics Agency (HESA) in the United Kingdom show that there were over 89,220 law postgraduates and undergraduates studying either full-time or part-time in the U.K. in the year 2013/14. This indicates a sharp rise of more than 60 % in the number of law students compared with two decades ago.[19] In contrast, academic staff has grown at a much slower rate which has inevitably resulted in increased teaching loads. Shortage of library space and supply of books is another concern which leads to growing needs in terms of resources and thus delays the introduction of new teaching technology.[20] Another reason for the reluctance to use new technology for law teaching purposes may stem from the fact that many educators have received no training and have little experience in this regard.[21]

1.2.3 Digital Age

The rapid expansion of technology has accelerated the speed and innovated the modes how information is disseminated. Technology has not only changed the modern way of life, but also teaching and learning cultures. Modern students are called 'digital natives'[22] with every reason.[23] Students of all disciplines nowadays grow up surrounded by technology. They use laptops, tablets, mobile phones, MP3, the Internet, Wi-Fi, YouTube, IM, Facebook, blogs to the extent that almost everything they do depends on technology. The convenience of technology has changed the way modern students learn—'[t]hey learn by doing, not by reading the instruction manual or listening to lectures.'[24] Modern students also often rely on online resources rather than printed materials when conducting legal research.[25]

Learning habits and learning preferences of modern students are very different from those of their educators who have not experienced a digitalized socialization.[26] While modern law teaching pedagogy still predominantly focuses on reading of printed textbooks, case books, statutes, educators all over the world have to face

[18]The Dearing Report, Section 3.4.

[19]Higher Education Statistics Agency (HESA) statistics. Compared with 52,700 law students in the year 1995/96. https://www.hesa.ac.uk/stats (last visited on 25 August 2015).

[20]Compare The Dearing Report, Section 3.60.

[21]The Dearing Report, 3.61.

[22]The term was introduced by Prensky, p. 2.

[23]Compare Gerdy/Wise/Craig, pp. 264–265; Oblinger, pp. 11–12 for discussion on digital natives' reliance on technology.

[24]McNeely, Section 4.3; compare Working Group for Distance learning in Legal Education ("Blue Paper"), p. 10.

[25]Lemmer, p. 469.

[26]Compare Matthew, pp. 48–49; Prensky, pp. 2–3.

the question how legal education can (or: has) to adapt to the habits of digital natives. Consequently, one major argument in favor of Flipped Classrooms is that the Flipped Classroom concept only mirrors the learning style of modern students.[27]

1.2.4 Legal Education and Technology

A number of academics have identified how the use of technology has improved or can improve law students' learning experience. As already indicated above,[28] for one thing technology can improve flexibility. Today, students no longer have to be at a particular place at a particular time to receive education. Instead, it is possible to allow them to choose between a synchronous setting, where participants are present at the same time (though not necessarily at the same location), or an asynchronous setting when the participants are not present at the same time, or place.[29] In addition, technology has varied the modes of delivery of education by means of different online tools. Examples of e-leaning tools are webcasts, video feeds/video link, podcasts, discussion forums, dialogs/chats, blogs, wikis, quizzes, and student's online assessment.[30] Increasingly common software programmes are so-called Learning Management Systems (LMS) or Internet-based Course Management Systems (CMS).[31] LMS and CMS allow teachers to upload digital teaching materials to the web for around the clock availability resulting in an increased and flexible access to education.[32] It is necessary for educators to understand the benefits and limitations of the available tools, including the Flipped Classroom concept, for the benefit of improved teaching strategies.[33]

1.3 Goals

Before the twenty-first century, course delivery either followed the traditional face-to-face format, where the teaching and interaction takes place inside class-rooms, or the pure online format, where the teaching and learning activities take place outside classrooms.[34] The Flipped Classroom concept is a new breed which

---

[27] *Infra*, 3.3.3.

[28] *Supra*, 1.2.1.

[29] Jones, p. 70; the Blue Paper, pp. 13–20. also see Hrastinski, pp. 51–52 for asynchronous and synchronous e-learning.

[30] For details on the recommended practices of technologies available, see Blue Paper.

[31] Note definitions of LMS and CMS may vary.

[32] Jones, p. 70; compare Blue Paper, pp. 19–20.

[33] Hrastinkski, p. 51.

[34] Hess, p. 51.

deviates from traditional concepts and which emerged in higher education in the last decade. It is a new approach which promotes learning supported by modern technology.[35] The Flipped Classroom model has become increasingly popular across various disciplines,[36] but only to a lesser extent in legal education.[37]

This book aims to reflect on the use of Flipped Classrooms from the viewpoint of legal education by:

- capturing the current status of the use of Flipped Classrooms in legal education;
- assessing the pedagogical viability of Flipped Classrooms in legal education;
- exploring the different forms of Flipped Classrooms;
- identifying different options to implement the Flipped Classroom concept and related advantages and disadvantages;
- considering technical and cost-related constraints of the Flipped Classroom concept; and
- reporting on a case study which adopted the Flipped Classroom concept for the course on 'The Law of International Business Transactions II'.

This book was originally planned to address Hong Kong specifics related to the use of Flipped Classrooms. As our work went along we had to discover that while Flipped Classrooms seem to be very popular there is not as much literature on the use of Flipped Classrooms in legal education as one would expect. As a result, our study had to address many very basic issues rather than just focusing on Hong Kong's situation. We trust that our study will therefore shed light on different aspects of Flipped Classrooms and hopefully be of general use. However, this book should be understood as a pilot study which attempts to explore Flipped Classrooms in its various dimensions. As such this book cannot and was never meant to offer comprehensive evidence, e.g. in the form of empirical data on the use of Flipped Classrooms. We hope that our work will establish the basis for related work of this kind in the future.

1.4 Methodology

Our research on Flipped Classrooms was originally designed as 'desk research'. We started with the collection of data to obtain a clear understanding of the terminology and conceptual underpinnings of the Flipped Classroom concept and the use of

---

[35] *Ibid.*

[36] Bonk/Kim/Zeng, p. 553.

[37] Among the websites of law schools searched, which are listed *infra* in Appendix A, eight law schools in the U.K. have either offered courses or articles published on Flipped Classrooms or blended learning. 20 of the law schools in the U.S. have published articles, provided manual or training, organized conference or workshop or carried out experiments related to the topic. 20 law schools in Australia and New Zealand have either offered courses, articles published, held trainings or conferences on the topic. Five Asian law schools have either experimented or organized news forum on the topic.

modern technology in legal education as well as to establish a 'ready-to-use database'. The sources consulted included targeted legal educational journals, and other materials identified by way of online key-word searches such as 'flipped classroom', 'blended learning' and 'technology-enhanced legal education'. Library search has supplemented the literature review.[38]

Furthermore, to understand if and how Flipped Classrooms are used in the day-to-day practice of law schools across the globe the websites of law schools worldwide have been searched for related information as follows[39]:

- 59 U.K. law schools
- 102 U.S. law schools
- 31 Australian law schools plus 2 New Zealand law schools
- 19 Asian law schools

The websites of continental European law schools were not checked comprehensively due to capacity limits and language problems.

The findings were supplemented by information collected on an ad hoc basis during public seminars given by educational experts which the authors and their collaborators attended such as the seminars on Flipped Classrooms by National Taiwan University Prof. Benson Yeh in October 2014 and CUHK Pro-Vice Chancellor Prof. K.T. Hau and his colleagues in November 2014, feedback given by attendees of seminars given by team members and by informal discussions with legal educational experts such as Prof. Paul Maharg who visited the CUHK Faculty of Law in December 2014.

While our work developed we found that desk research alone would render our study somewhat incomplete. Consequently, in order to test and confirm the findings of our literature review, we conducted a case study. This case study, on which this book reports in its Chap. 6 and which is also meant to demonstrate how Flipped Classrooms can be developed in practice, entailed the 'flipping' of teaching modules of the CUHK Faculty of Law course on 'The Law of Cross-border Business Transactions II' (LIBT II).

1.5 Structure

This book is structured as follows:

Chapter 2 develops a definition of 'Flipped Classrooms' adopted for the purpose of this book on the basis of a comprehensive literature review. Chapter 3 discusses the pedagogical viability of Flipped Classrooms in legal education. Chapter 4

---

[38]See *infra*, 'References'.

[39]For details see *infra*, Appendix A.

explains practical aspects of the development of Flipped Classrooms for legal educational purposes. Chapter 5 addresses related costs. Chapter 6 describes as a case study the development of a framework for the use of Flipped Classrooms for the LIBT II course as well as the implementation of this framework by way of a pilot scheme. Chapter 7 concludes the book with a Summary and Final Remarks.

Chapter 2
Defining Flipped Classrooms

2.1 General

The term 'Flipped Classroom' does not carry a technical meaning and is not used uniformly. We have conducted a literature review with the ultimate goal to develop a terminological and conceptual framework for this book as set out in the following sections.

2.2 Literature Review

2.2.1 Flipped Classrooms

There is no universal definition of the term 'Flipped Classroom'.[1] However, it appears that academics agree that a flipped classroom generally provides pre-recorded lectures (video or audio) followed by in-class activities. Students view the videos outside the classroom before or after coming to class where the freed time can be devoted to interactive modules such as Q&A sessions, discussions, exercises or other learning activities.[2] Since Flipped Classrooms 'invert' activities inside the classroom with activities outside the classroom, they are sometimes also referred to as 'inverted' classrooms.[3]

The origins of Flipped Classrooms can be traced back to 2007 when two high school chemistry teachers in Colorado, Jonathan Bergmann and Aaron Sams, became concerned with students who often missed classes to attend 'competitions,

[1]CADQ, p. 1, quoting Schell who reckons that under the Flipped Classroom model, 'there is no prescribed set of rules to follow or approach to fit'.
[2]Compare Educause, p. 1; CADQ, p. 1; Lihosit/Larrington, p. 1; Davis/Neary/Vaughn, p. 13; Slomanson, p. 95; Upchurch, p. 1; Wood.
[3]Lemmer, p. 463.

L.-C. Wolff and J. Chan, *Flipped Classrooms for Legal Education*,
SpringerBriefs in Law, DOI 10.1007/978-981-10-0479-7_2

games or other events'.[4] They began to record lectures, demonstrations and slide presentations which they then posted on YouTube for students to access.[5]

Since then Flipped Classrooms have evolved into a number of variations all with video lectures as their key feature. Sometimes the video lectures include embedded questions prepared by the instructor and students are required to read background materials or participate in online quizzes before coming to class.[6] Some Flipped Classroom models use audio recording instead of video recording.[7]

2.2.2 *Blended Learning and Hybrid Learning*

The Flipped Classroom model shares similar features with another increasingly popular learning mode, i.e. 'blended learning', which is also called 'hybrid learning'. Flipped Classrooms and blended learning are similar in that they share on-and off-campus components.[8] According to Beck, 'the terms "hybrid" and "blended" have typically been used interchangeably' and both approaches feature traditional face-to-face and internet-based elements.[9] Similar to Flipped Classrooms, there is no universal understanding or definition of 'blended learning'.[10] Means et al. in carrying out a study on online learning for the U.S. Department of Education distinguish between 'blended learning' and 'pure online learning'. They point out that 'blended learning' includes 'face-to-face instruction to provide learning enhancement'[11]

Means et al's definition also clarifies the key difference between Flipped Classrooms or 'blended learning' on the one hand and purely online teaching models such as Massive Open Online Courses (MOOCs) which are becoming very popular across the world.[12] In the Flipped Classroom and 'blended learning' modes, video or audio lectures are often uploaded to the internet to facilitate viewing. This is of course normally also the case in purely online teaching models. However, under a purely online teaching model learning is conducted entirely off-site. In contrast, Flipped Classrooms and 'blended learning' modes combine both in-class and out-of-class learning. Video lectures are added for the purpose of 'enhancing' or 'supplementing' in-class learning.[13] In contrast, face-to-face learning is unavailable under a purely online teaching setting.

---

[4]Hamdan/McKnight/Afstrom, p. 3.

[5]*Ibid.*

[6]Davis/Neary/Vaughn, p. 13.

[7]CADQ, p. 2; Educase, p. 1.

[8]Hess, p. 56.

[9]Beck, p. 274, footnote 1.

[10]Polding, p. 3.

[11]Means/Toyama/Murphy/Bakia/Jones, p. 9.

[12]Compare Slomanson, p. 94.

[13]Hess, p. 55.

Graham in his effort to define 'blended learning' clarifies that 'blended learning' is not about combining instructional methods or media, as defining 'blended learning' by these two ways would include almost all learning systems and 'water down' the essence of this concept.[14] According to his working definition 'blended learning systems combine face-to-face instruction with computer-mediated instruction.'[15] He clarifies that 'blended learning' has combined two historically separated teaching and learning systems, i.e. 'traditional face-to-face learning systems and distributed learning systems' with the emphasis on the 'role of computer-based technologies in blended learning'.[16]

Macdonald's survey of 'blended learning' at universities in the U.K. revealed that most respondents describe 'blended learning' by its two most common components, i.e. 'asynchronous forums and face-to-face contact'.[17] Instead of using video/audio lecture formats, the asynchronous forms are used for tutor-mediated learning or peer support, by means of tools such as email, telephone, real-time chat and whiteboards.[18] Face-to-face contact takes the form of tutorials, seminars, demonstrations in labs or lectures. In some cases, video-conferencing might be used to replace lectures.[19]

Ireland agrees that there is no universal definition for 'blended learning'. She proposes that 'broadly speaking, blended learning can be used to refer to any teaching method that blends online and offline elements.'[20] The way Ireland designed her 'blended learning' activities resembles Flipped Classrooms. She used podcasts to substitute about half of the face-to-face in-class time.[21] Seminars were chosen for the face-to-face components to provide opportunity for students to practice oral and aural skills and to engage in problem-solving techniques.[22]

While a clear distinction between the Flipped Classroom concept and 'blended learning' models is not attempted by most authors it appears that 'blended learning' models are often understood as being more flexible in the choice of technological tools than Flipped Classrooms. For example, Field and Jones have not used only video lectures but also engaged in a wide range of other activities to blend their courses. Examples are multiple choice tests, short answers, mini-research questions,

---

14 Graham, p. 4.

15 *Ibid*, p. 5.

16 *Ibid*.

17 Macdonald, p. 33.

18 *Ibid*.

19 *Ibid*. pp. 33–34.

20 Ireland, p. 140.

21 *Ibid*, pp. 140–141.

22 *Ibid*, p. 141.

full length essay and problem questions.[23] In contrast, the 'blended learning' model adopted by Catley only included classroom coursework and online quizzes.[24]

As one of the few authors who has actually attempted to distinguish between Flipped Classrooms and 'blended learning', Hess focused on whether the online instruction is additional to or replaces the face-to-face classes. According to his definition, in Flipped Classrooms students can acquire content online via short video lectures.[25] 'The subsequent class session focuses on application, problem solving, analysis, and other active methods to deepen student learning'.[26] For Hess Flipped Classrooms do not replace face-to-face teaching with online instruction.[27] Instead, it is the goal of Flipped Classrooms to free up in-class time for interactive learning activities of different types.[28] In contrast, in a 'blended learning' model the online learning activity replaces some of the in-class time.[29]

Video lectures are sometimes used as a teaching tool without branding it as Flipped Classrooms or as 'blended learning'. McKellar and Maharg used video lectures when teaching Civil and Criminal Procedure in the Diploma in Legal Practice at the Glasgow Graduate School of Law, Strathclyde University.[30] The video lectures and face-to-face tutorials were combined as part of an integrated course of study.[31]

To sum up, our literature review shows that there is no unified terminological and conceptual understanding of Flipped Classrooms and 'blended learning'. Both models take a variety of formats. The term 'blended learning' appears to stand for models across a wide spectrum and may or may not include video lectures. Flipped Classrooms are normally seen as blending e-learning with classroom learning. From this viewpoint Flipped Classrooms could be categorized as one branch of 'blended learning'.[32]

2.2.3 Podcasting

Podcasting has become a very popular choice of technology to distribute digital media files (in video or audio format) for playback on portable media players.[33]

---

[23]See Field/Jones, p. 384.

[24]Catley, p. 4 under 'Initial thoughts about e-learning'; p. 6 under 'Stage 2: Introducing WebCT-based quizzes'.

[25]Hess, p. 56.

[26]*Ibid.*

[27]*Ibid.*

[28]*Ibid.*

[29]*Ibid.*

[30]McKellar/Maharg, p. 44.

[31]Compare *ibid,* pp. 43–45.

[32]Compare Lemmer, p. 466.

[33]Brittain/Glowaki/Van Ittersum/Johnson, p. 25.

Podcasting has become increasingly popular in universities. Duke University 'passed out free iPods to its entire freshman class in the fall of 2004'.[34] Yale, MIT, Purdue, Stanford and UC Berkeley have as well used video and audio lectures.[35] According to Lonn and Teasley podcasting was a choice mostly for universities that had taken a forward looking advanced approach in using modern technology.[36] Rather than replacing lectures with online materials students used podcasts as review materials to prepare for quizzes and exams.[37] Lonn and Teasley point out that there is disagreement regarding the effect of podcasting on learning. 'For example, students in business and dentistry reported that using podcasts helped them revise their notes more effectively than using the textbook…Several studies have shown that podcasting has a similar effect on student learning as other review materials.'[38] Another study found that 'students only benefited from podcasts if they took notes, listened to the podcast several times, and generally behaved similarly to the way they already do during lecture sessions.'[39]

To sum up, podcasting is an e-learning tool used as additional learning resource. Podcasting is not aimed to replace in-class lectures and from this viewpoint podcasting does not compete with, i.e. is not in the same category like Flipped Classrooms or 'blended learning'.

2.3 Definition Adopted for This Book

There is no unified understanding/definition of the concept of Flipped Classrooms (and the connected concept of 'blended learning') in legal education. Our cursory research suggests that the same is true in other areas. It goes without saying that these terminological and conceptual uncertainties make comparisons and informed discussions unnecessarily difficult. For this book it was therefore crucial to adopt a definition which is in line with the common conceptual understanding of Flipped Classrooms. For this book the term 'Flipped Classroom(s)' shall therefore stand for any teaching model which replaces in-class lecture modules with video or audio lectures with the goal to use the freed in-class time for interactivity.

---

[34]Lonn/Teasely, pp. 88–89.

[35]*Ibid.*

[36]*Ibid,* p. 91.

[37]*Ibid.*

[38]*Ibid*, p. 89.

[39]*Ibid.*

Chapter 3
The Pedagogical Feasibility of Flipped Classrooms

3.1 General

The benefit of using technology on education was already mentioned above[1] and has been widely documented.[2] However, although Flipped Classrooms have become increasingly popular, the concept is relatively new.[3] The question of course is, if Flipped Classrooms offer distinct pedagogical advantages which outweigh any actual and potential disadvantages. The following sections discuss this and related questions on the basis of a comprehensive literature review.

We first report potential disadvantages of the traditional lecture concept. Then, we discuss specific advantages of Flipped Classrooms which have been identified by others against the background of the traditional lecture concept. More specifically we analyse if and how the Socratic Method and Flipped Classrooms relate to each other. We then discuss video flipping versus audio flipping. In the final part of this section we point to general observations and open questions.

It is important that contrary to our expectations for the following sections we were not able to rely on much specific literature on the use of Flipped Classrooms in legal education. As a consequence we had to rely not only on studies on Flipped Classrooms, but also on reports on blended learning in general for both legal education and other disciplines. Furthermore, studies which attempt to produce or have actually produced hard evidence in the form of reliable empirical data on the use of Flipped Classrooms are rare[4] and it is consequently difficult to come to conclusions which go beyond general observations based just on the existing literature.

---

[1] *Supra*, 1.2.4.
[2] Compare only Gerdy/Wise/Craig, pp. 271–273; Jones, p. 72; Bloxham, p. 100.
[3] Compare *supra*, 1.3.
[4] Compare Newman, p. 195.

L.-C. Wolff and J. Chan, *Flipped Classrooms for Legal Education*,
SpringerBriefs in Law, DOI 10.1007/978-981-10-0479-7_3

3.2 Arguments Contra Traditional Lectures

3.2.1 General

It is an implied theme of any discussion of the Flipped Classroom concept that the traditional lecture model is not a suitable way of teaching law, at least if it is not combined with interactive modules. In this section, we discuss arguments put forward to support this assumption.

3.2.2 Is Traditional Lecture an Effective Law Teaching Method?

Le Brun and Johnstone explain in their groundbreaking book on the need of reforms of legal education that the principal mode of legal education in Australia was lecturing.[5] A typical lecture in Australia entails a one-way discourse of information from teachers to students for 50 minutes.[6] Although lecturing has the advantages of being cheap and potentially less demanding as it requires little interaction between teachers and students,[7] the advantages may be outweighed by its disadvantages. Lectures fail to deliver an active learning environment. When placed in the lecture setting, students' learning activity is reduced to 'note-taking'.[8] Lectures also do not engage students in any interaction with teachers.[9] Lecturing may even compromise learning as the limited interaction prevents teachers from assessing the students' understanding. Students may misinterpret the content of the lecture without teachers knowing it.[10]

Le Brun and Johnstone explain that learning is not about transfer of knowledge, but rather it is a process of construction based on what the learners already know.[11] Sustainable knowledge requires internalization. In contrast, to ensure effective learning, 'information must be embedded in an organising structure.'[12] Thus teaching requires more than just transmitting information, but must give priority to assist learners to construct their own knowledge.[13]

Donahoe's experience on how to teach modern students is in line with these findings. He purports that modern students need their learning to be 'three-dimensional'.[14]

---

[5]Le Brun/Johnstone, p. 257. Note that the book was published in 1994.

[6]*Ibid.*

[7]*Ibid*, p. 258.

[8]*Ibid*, p. 257.

[9]*Ibid.*

[10]*Ibid*, p. 258.

[11]*Ibid*, p. 71.

[12]*Ibid*, p. 71, discussing Resnick's theories.

[13]*Ibid*,

[14]Donahoe, p. 488.

They learn by participating in the process. He recalls his lecturing experience by using PowerPoint slides and finds that this technology did not stimulate students but rather put them to the backseat.[15] He concludes that modern students are self-directed and do not find passively listening to lectures engaging at all.[16]

Lectures are effective in conveying information quickly and concisely, especially when the information is difficult to gather by other means or requires reorganization.[17] However, there seems to be agreement that one should avoid using lectures as the sole teaching mode simply for one reason, namely lecturing succeeds in achieving low-order learning activities such as knowledge and comprehension but it scores poorly in 'stimulating thought or fostering higher-level abilities.'[18]

Le Brun and Johnstone recommend teachers to provide students with notes, handouts or references to textbooks instead of lecturing for the sheer purpose of conveying information.[19] They also warn against replacing reading with lecturing.[20] As a matter of fact, as skills required by the legal profession, such as application, analysis and evaluation, often lie in the higher-order learning activities, teachers should limit their use of lectures.[21] This is far from saying that teachers should refrain completely from using lectures. Lectures still possess value in conveying information.[22] And, other teaching methods can compensate for the pedagogical shortcomings of lectures. Bligh explains in this regard that teachers often have a number of teaching objectives and different objectives should be achieved by different methods.[23]

Appleby's discussion of his teaching experience may explain why lectures alone are insufficient teaching modes and why sometimes a combination of different teaching methods is essential. Appleby when teaching 'The Politics of Law' combined lectures with discussions.[24] He believes that this teaching strategy was able to foster critical thinking.[25] He divided the three-hour weekly session into one hour of lecturing and two hours of discussion.[26] Quoting the definition offered by the Critical Thinking Community, he explains that critical thinking should entail 'the art of analyzing and evaluating thinking with the view to improving it'.[27] Appleby admits that the teaching of law often requires a transmission of vast

---

[15] *Ibid*, p. 490.

[16] *Ibid*, p. 487.

[17] Compare Le Brun/Johnstone, p. 259.

[18] *Ibid*.

[19] *Ibid*.

[20] *Ibid*.

[21] *Ibid*, pp. 259–260, 266.

[22] *Ibid*, p. 264.

[23] Bligh, p. 228.

[24] Appleby/Burdon/Reilly, p. 364.

[25] *Ibid*.

[26] *Ibid*.

[27] *Ibid*, p. 347.

amount of information such as 'the legal institutions of the state, the origins of the common law and Australian legal systems, the political processes that generate laws, the systems of dispute resolution, and a knowledge of key areas of legal doctrine and their application'.[28] But teachers should not easily resort to lecturing just because the teaching load is heavy,[29] since putting students at the recipient end of information does not promote critical thinking at all. Instead, as 'there is a direct link between independent learning and critical thinking',[30] teachers should create a learning environment to encourage self-directed learning.[31]

Appleby's understanding of critical thinking is reflected in his course design. Before the term started, he delivered the course description in a handout to provide students guidance on how to read texts critically and explained why critical thinking is important to the course.[32] In the first session, he also specified that preliminary reading is required before coming to class.[33] The 'dominant method of teaching' was group discussion.[34] At the end of every session, Appleby asked students to prepare answers to questions prior to the next class.[35] These questions stood in the center of the group discussions. Students were asked to present their own answers and to comment on the views of their counterparts.[36] The purpose of lectures according to Appleby is to supplement discussion to model the forms of 'democratic dispositions'.[37]

3.2.3 Current Practice in the U.K., Canada and Australia

Despite any acknowledged disadvantages, lecturing remains the predominant teaching method in the U.K.,[38] Canada[39] and Australia.[40] The 'old U.K. universities' tend to deliver more hours of lectures than the 'new U.K. universities'.[41]

---

[28]*Ibid*, p. 362.

[29]*Ibid*.

[30]*Ibid*, p. 363.

[31]*Ibid*, p. 363.

[32]*Ibid*, pp. 364–365.

[33]*Ibid*, p. 365.

[34]*Ibid*.

[35]*Ibid*, pp. 365–366.

[36]*Ibid*. p. 366.

[37]*Ibid*.

[38]Harris/Beinart, p. 315.

[39]Rochette, p. 176.

[40]LeBrun/Johnstone, p. 258; compare *supra*, 3.2.2.

[41]Harris/Beinart, p. 315.

Rochette explains that legal education in Canada demonstrates weakness in the development of higher level learning. She conducted a survey on how Canadian law teachers are teaching law and found that lecturing dominates, supplemented by occasional discussions or the Socratic Method.[42] She observed that lecturing may not be the most appropriate teaching method to acquire higher level critical thinking skills.[43] When asked how students should be taught to be critical thinkers, teachers often struggled to find an answer and eventually managed to respond that they achieve the goal by assigning critical content reading materials, various evaluation methods or by lecturing or asking questions in class.[44] According to Rochette it is possible that there is a disconnect between the educational goals and teaching methods teachers use in Canadian classrooms.[45]

In Australia small-group teaching was introduced for a short while before it was replaced by lecturing again.[46] Thornton blames the shortage of financial resources and students' desire for pre-packaged lectures for the quick return to lecture-based pedagogy.[47] In fact, according to one dean, teaching small groups would require twice the teaching time.[48] Thornton also explains that the lecture method is efficient from the perspective of both, teachers and students. Lectures allow teachers to teach 500 students simultaneously and if recorded, enable online transmission to many more.[49] Prolonged lecture hours are often well-received by students as it means that less in-class presence is required.[50] Given the amount of coverage of information required by the admitting authorities, lecturing appears to be the rational choice for a one-way 'transmission of pre-packaged knowledge for recording, memorizing and regurgitation'.[51]

According to interviews conducted with teaching staff, students seldom seemed to appreciate the educational values of in-class interaction or other initiatives to engage students in critical thinking.[52] According to Thornton interactive learning is even less well-received by non-law students, who only have general ideas on law and do not always have a critical perspective as legal students do.[53]

---

42 Rochette, p. 176.

43 *Ibid.*

44 *Ibid*, p. 190.

45 *Ibid*, p. 191.

46 Thornton, p. 86.

47 *Ibid*, p. 87.

48 *Ibid*, p. 89.

49 *Ibid*, p. 86.

50 *Ibid.*

51 *Ibid*, p. 87.

52 *Ibid*, pp. 88–90.

53 *Ibid*, p. 88.

3.2.4 Defending Lectures

Some academics suggest that proper lecturing requires more than 'merely standing before a class and talking'.[54] In contrast, when performed correctly, lectures can deliver distinct educational benefits.[55]

Exley and Dennick emphasize that lectures add variety to teaching methods. Any curriculum that includes multiple learning outcomes requires different teaching methods to succeed.[56] The use of lectures can ensure a balance with other teaching methods and benefit students with different learning styles.[57] McLeish, in his investigation of the effectiveness of lectures, studied a number of surveys conducted by other academics. Many of these surveys suggest that lectures could be an effective way to teach when done in an appropriate manner.[58] A study by Marr et al. confirms that students who attend courses delivered in the lecture format scored marginally higher in the examination compared with those who attended Q&A sessions with the same teacher.[59] McLeish quotes Beach's findings that 'introverts performed better than extraverts in the lecture and class discussion groups (instructor present) whereas the reverse was true in the autonomous groups'.[60]

Another benefit of lecturing is seen in the fact that it allows explanations by teachers.[61] Hativa has pointed out that the most valuable properties of lectures are 'clarity, interest, logical organization, selection of appropriate content, eliciting responses from students, focusing attention upon important points, relevance to students, use of examples and illustrations, use of diagrams and enthusiasm.'[62] However, the task of explaining may sound easier than it actually is. Garlikov has addressed the difficulties in making a good explanation. Teachers often miss key steps, making it difficult for students to follow.[63] While explanations by too many steps will get students bored, too few steps may make it difficult for students to keep up. The more complex and abstract subjects are the more difficult it becomes to provide good explanations.[64]

Generally speaking, the educational value of teaching modes which encourage students to find answers themselves is higher than those where someone else develops answers for and communicates them to students. The independent

---

[54]Henderson/Nash, pp. 34–35; Hativa, p. 72.

[55]Note that literature cited in the following is not legal education related, but general or related to other disciplines.

[56]Exley/Dennick, p. 3.

[57]*Ibid*, p. 5.

[58]McLeish, p. 47.

[59]*Ibid*, p. 40.

[60]*Ibid*, p. 43.

[61]Henderson/Nash, p. 35; compare Hativa, p. 81.

[62]Hativa, p. 84.

[63]See Garlikov under 'Interpreting an Experience Versus Experiencing an Interpretation'.

[64]Compare *ibid*.

identification of questions and the development of related answers imply an active learning process while waiting for someone else to explain the answer is a passive one.[65] However, there are two situations that make explanations valuable. The first is when students have unsuccessfully tried to answer a question. It obviously helps them to hear and consider someone else's explanation.[66] The second situation is when teachers try to explain something through a 'guided discovery … in such a way that students can anticipate what comes next, while then internalizing or absorbing what came before …'.[67]

According to studies conducted by McLeish and Thielens no reading can replace good lectures.[68] This is because no amount of textbook or reading can understand the needs and ability of students better than teachers.[69] Teachers can input most up-to-date information which cannot be available in reading materials.[70] By adopting a particular lecture style teachers can cater to the particular needs of their students.[71] Teachers can repeat explanations in different ways to improve the comprehension.[72] Lectures allow teachers an opportunity to use visual aids to enhance their teaching.[73] Maintaining the human touch in lectures improves the learning atmosphere.[74]

Light et al. defend lecturing with the argument that lectures can be engaging if teachers choose to enter into a dialogue with students[75] instead of carrying out a monotonous speech. Hativa agrees that if used together with other teaching methods, good lectures could in fact promote active learning.[76]

It is important that the definition of lectures used by Hativa and Light et al. goes beyond the traditional narrow definition of lectures which entails nothing more than an uninterrupted transmission of information from teachers to students. The model these academics promote implies a wider definition of lectures which comprise a face-to-face session which combines traditional lecture with teacher-centered Q&A modules.

It is also apparent that some teachers are more successful in using lectures than others.[77] According to Light et al., the reason for distinction is hardly related to the

[65] *Ibid.*

[66] Compare *ibid.*

[67] *Ibid.*

[68] Hativa, p. 79.

[69] *Ibid.*

[70] *Ibid*, p. 80.

[71] *Ibid*, Compare with McLeish, p. 47. McLeish held the view that lectures pay little regard to the individual learning needs.

[72] *Ibid.*

[73] *Ibid.*

[74] *Ibid.*

[75] Light/Cox/Calkins, p. 109.

[76] Hativa, pp. 76, 87–110.

[77] Light/Cox/Calkins, p. 108.

content they teach or their personality, but to the way teachers choose to deliver the content.[78] Light et al. argue that the key to success is the enthusiasm of teachers to engage students in a meaningful dialogue, in giving a lecture that draws on the experience of students so as to help them achieve deeper learning.[79]

Gottfredson et al. believe that students' learning experience can be improved as long as teachers make an effort to improve it. He admits that the stress level of legal studies may be high.[80] As long as law students feel a sense of belonging and engagement in meaningful work, even the most stressed law students may also be the ones with the highest level of life satisfaction.[81] Gottfredson et al. conducted a student survey based on Diener et al.'s five-item 'Satisfaction with Life-scale' to assess law students' well-being.[82] The five-item scales include (1) 'school characteristics', (2) 'individual demographic characteristics and personality', (3) 'social support', (4) 'perceived academic efficacy', (5) 'engagement with/meaningfulness of course material'.[83] Participants were 6100 incoming law students from 50 countries.[84] On the fifth scale, students valued 'perceived quality of instruction' and 'perceived quality of class discussions', indicating that both are positively related to life satisfaction.[85]

3.2.5 The SAMR Model

Saliba et al. used Puentedura's SAMR model to explain how integrating technology into teaching can lead to high-level learning outcomes.[86] The SAMR model is intended to help teachers to decide which online components to employ when they design their blended learning strategy. The SAMR model consists of four levels of functions, i.e Substitution, Augmentation, Modification and Redefinition.[87] Substitution is the lowest level of function where technology is used as a tool to substitute teaching without functional improvement.[88] Augmentation is the second level where some functional improvement is added to the teaching through the use of technology.[89] At the Modification level, the primary task remains the same, but

---

[78] *Ibid*, pp. 108–109.
[79] Compare *ibid.*, p. 111.
[80] Gottfredson/Panter/Daye/Allen/Wightman/Deo, p. 521.
[81] *Ibid*, pp. 520–521.
[82] *Ibid*, p. 524.
[83] *Ibid.*
[84] *Ibid*, p. 523.
[85] *Ibid*, p. 526.
[86] Saliba/Rankine/Cortez, p. 13.
[87] *Ibid*, Fig. 1.
[88] *Ibid*, p. 14.
[89] *Ibid.*

the use of technology enhances productivity substantially.[90] The highest level, Redefinition, engages technology with the goal to redesign the task.[91] The higher the level teaching activities are at, the more sophisticated is the required planning. According to this model, flipping the classroom may be equivalent to using technology at a substitution level because video lectures are used to 'substitute' face-to-face lectures.[92]

Hence, if teaching inevitably requires conveying a large amount of pre-packaged information, and if one accepts that lecturing is a quick and precise transmission of knowledge while precious in-class time should be reserved for interactive teaching, it may indeed be advantageous to deliver lectures to students outside the classroom as it is suggested by the Flipped Classroom model.

3.3 Arguments Pro Flipped Classrooms

3.3.1 Improved Learning Experience

A number of authors suggest that Flipped Classrooms and blended learning techniques in legal education lead to improved learning experiences. Particular advantages are seen in the possibility to promote active learning, to increase interaction between faculty and students, to improve the collaboration among students, to allow flexible learning just-in-time and to foster critical thinking.[93]

Davis et al. have observed this after the introduction of Flipped Classrooms in their Advance Legal Research (ALR) course.[94] As students spend more class time on hands-on legal research, they become more active and responsible learners engaging in their own studies.[95] Davis et al. had decided to use the Flipped Classroom concept for the ALR course and some other practice-specific courses[96] to facilitate constant practice and simulation.[97] The Flipped Classrooms allowed freeing-up classroom time once the lecture content was shifted to video delivery with the ultimate goal to promote active learning by increasing in-class interactivity.[98] Prior to class, students were supposed to view videos supplemented by

[90] *Ibid.*

[91] *Ibid.*

[92] Compare, *ibid*, p. 24.

[93] Compare Beck; CADQ; Gerdy/Wise/Craig; Hamdan/McKnight/Afstrom; Hess; Davis/Neary/Vaughn; Lemmer; Lihosit/Larrington; McKellar/Maharg; Slomanson; Upchurch; Wood.

[94] Davis/Neary/Vaughn, at Boston College of Law School, academic year 2012/13.

[95] Compare *ibid*, pp. 16–17.

[96] *Ibid*, p. 13, footnote 1.

[97] *Ibid*, p. 13.

[98] *Ibid.*

reading assignments, online quizzes and the work on assigned research problems.[99] More time could be allocated to 'analyzing complex hypotheticals and crafting effective research strategies' which in turn helped students' deep learning experience.[100] The feedback from teaching staff was positive. For example, they reported that students began to ask more complicated legal questions.[101] Flipped Classrooms also improved student collaboration through discussions, demonstrations or presentations. When students were working in a group, they mirrored the situation of lawyers collaborating with each other to find a solution.[102] Flipped Classrooms also increased the interaction between faculty and students thus helping teachers to conduct discussions more effectively.[103] By working side by side with students, teachers were able to observe any common areas of confusion and address the issue on the spot which helped to deepen students' understanding.[104]

Slomanson flipped the Civil Procedure course offered at the Thomas Jefferson School of Law with the goal to free up in-class time for simulation group exercises.[105] Slomanson concluded that Flipped Classrooms allow for more time to teach students upper-level skills useful for their future career and also improved both faculty-student interaction and peer collaboration.[106] The more structured questions which students asked in-class confirmed that viewing contents before class helped them understand the topic better.[107] Students' survey responses confirmed this conclusion.[108]

Verkerke flipped a first-year contract law course offered at the University of Virginia which had previously been taught solely by using the Socratic Method.[109] He redesigned his course and moved contents that do not require the Socratic dialogue to pre-recorded lectures in order to free in-class time for problem-solving exercises and small-group discussions.[110] According to Verkerke's experience unlike the traditional Socratic classroom[111] where only a small number of students participated in the Q&A, the newly introduced exercises engaged most of the

[99] *Ibid.*

[100] *Ibid*, p. 16.

[101] *Ibid*, p. 17.

[102] *Ibid*, p. 16.; compare also Boyle/Dunn, p. 231.

[103] *Ibid*, p. 19.

[104] *Ibid*, p. 17.

[105] Slomanson, p. 95.

[106] *Ibid*, pp. 100–101.

[107] *Ibid*, pp. 101–102.

[108] *Ibid*,

[109] See Wood citing an interview of Professor Verkerke about his Flipped Classroom experience.

[110] *Ibid.*

[111] Compare *infra*, 3.4.2.

students.[112] He observed that students who participated in the exercises engaged in deep thinking and felt empowered by reporting their findings to the entire class.[113]

Active learning, peer collaboration, faculty and student interaction, i.e. core features of the Flipped Classroom concept, are critical components of the 'Seven Principles of Good Practice in Undergraduate Education' developed by Chickering and Gamson to help teachers in higher education to facilitate teaching.[114]

3.3.2 Flexible Learning

One obvious benefit of Flipped Classrooms is convenience and flexibility. This suits the learning needs of digital native students[115] who can in principle access learning resources whenever and wherever.[116] Slomanson found that the flexibility offered by the video lecture allows students to study at their own pace, leading to greater ownership of their learning.[117] In fact, the improved access to higher education brought by technological advancements is widely regarded as an important aspect of modern education.[118] Bloxham holds the view that increasing access and e-learning has a positive effect on students' learning experience and good retention rates.[119] Data from the University of Central Florida show that student retention in blended learning courses is higher than that in courses delivered purely online or in the face-to-face mode.[120]

Nevertheless, it has also been pointed out that with the increase in flexibility, students can acquire their knowledge without attending any class which may result in a reduced face-to-face classroom attendance.[121] Once students familiarize themselves with the technology used and the experience of learning online, they may feel that they no longer need to attend classes.[122] The blended model tested in a course on Intellectual Property Law offered at the University of Western Sydney contests these concerns.[123] Ireland has explained in this regard that the attendance

---

[112]Wood.

[113]*Ibid.*

[114]Jones, pp. 77–78. The seven principles are: 'Encourage contact between students and faculty. Develop reciprocity and cooperation among students. Encourage active learning. Give prompt feedback. Emphasize time on task. Communicate high expectation. Respect diverse talents and ways of learning'.

[115]Donahoe, p. 491. *Supra*, 1.2.3.

[116]CADQ, p. 2.

[117]Slomanson, p. 97.

[118]Dziuban/Moskal, p. 236.

[119]Bloxham, p. 93.

[120]Moskal/Dziuban/Hartman, p. 18.

[121]Traphagan/Kucsera/Kishi, p. 34.

[122]Bos/Groeneveld/Bruggen/Brand-Gruwel, p. 9.

[123]Ireland, p. 146. The course was offered in the summer session of 2008.

rate is closely related to the course design. If the contents of face-to-face teaching sessions differ from the podcast content and teaching sessions are not recorded for later podcasting attendance should not be a problem.[124] Since the face-to-face teaching sessions contained 'examinable material and exam practice', they retained their importance and the blended model seemed to have little effect on the attendance rate.[125] The results of an empirical study conducted in relation to a non-legal blended course confirm this assessment. They suggest that it is the grade point average and credit hours transferred from previous institutions, rather than the teaching mode that have positive and significant influence on students' attendance.[126]

3.3.3 IT Literacy

The Flipped Classroom model is not only an effective way of learning. In contrast, this new model can also teach students information technology (IT) literacy which is crucial for success in the modern legal profession.[127] Lemmer stresses that in a world where IT literacy is increasingly important, it is necessary to teach future lawyers how to use search engines, online databases and knowledge management tools.[128] In the fall semester of 2012, she flipped her LL.M. legal research class which covers general U.S. legal topics.[129] She used avatars, animated texts for legal research presentations, embedded quizzes and short exercises in the tutorial videos.[130] As an additional feature students were allowed to index slides for future viewing.[131] Pettys concludes that 'the technology enables professors to be much more creative in their efforts to convey information in a manner aimed at awakening student interest and laying the foundations for higher-level analytic work.'[132]

3.3.4 Improved Learning Outcomes

In the previous sections we have focused on observations regarding students' learning experience. However, a number of studies suggest that students' improved

---

[124]*Ibid*, p. 156.

[125]*Ibid*, pp. 156–157.

[126]Asarta/Schimdt, p. 30.

[127]Compare Lemmer, p. 466.

[128]*Ibid*, p. 487.

[129]*Ibid*, p. 488.

[130]*Ibid*, p. 490.

[131]*Ibid.*

[132]Pettys, p. 1309.

learning experience also has positive effects on learning outcomes.[133] In fact, the improved learning outcomes of blended courses as compared with traditional classroom teaching and courses which are delivered completely online have been documented by some authors as highlighted in the following.[134]

Upchurch adopted the Flipped Classroom approach in teaching Civil Procedure offered by the Capital University Law School in 2012.[135] Upchurch concludes that Flipped Classrooms do not only accomplish more teaching goals.[136] In contrast, Flipped Classrooms also help to 'close the gap between the strongest and weakest students in the class' and improve the class performance as a whole.[137] According to Upchurch, 'students were consistently out-performing prior classes on objective assessments' and on the final exam.[138]

More extensive studies have been done in relation to non-legal education.[139] Means et al. when conducting empirical studies on behalf of the U.S. Department of Education, collected data with the aim to improve online learning for K–12 education and teacher preparation.[140] The meta-analysis revealed that blended courses had higher success rates than pure online or face-to-face courses.[141] Data from the University of Central Florida also confirm that students who participate in blended courses scored better in terms of success, attendance and withdrawal rates than their peers in the face-to-face or courses delivered solely online.[142]

According to an empirical survey in non-legal studies conducted by Owston et al. (2013), high achievers achieved better learning outcomes through blended learning modes.[143] However, the same could not be said about low achievers.[144] Owston et al. (2013) therefore suggest giving students a choice whether to enroll in blended or face-to-face course, especially in more difficult subject areas.[145]

---

[133]Compare Ginns/Ellis, pp. 62–63; apparently different Lopez-Perez/Pérez-López/Rodríguez-Ariza, p. 824.

[134]Compare Beck; Bloxham; CADQ; Donahoe; Gerdy/Wise/Craig; Davis/Neary/Vaughn; Lemmer; Lihosit/Larrington; Means/Toyama/Murphy/Bakia/Jones; Moskal/Dziuban/Hartman; McKella/Maharg; Owston/York/Murtha (2013); Upchurch.

[135]Upchurch, p. 1.

[136]*Ibid*, p. 3.

[137]*Ibid.*

[138]*Ibid.*

[139]Means/Toyama/Murphy/Bakia/Jones, p. 30. The studies cover K-12, undergraduate and graduate education and also a wide range of subjects.

[140]*Ibid*, p. 2.

[141]*Ibid*, pp. 18–19.

[142]Moskal/Dziuban/Hartman, p. 18.

[143]Owston/York/Murtha, p. 43.

[144]*Ibid.*

[145]*Ibid.*

3.3.5 Students' Feedback

Is the Flipped Classroom model well received by students? Evaluation results in relation to the Flipped Classroom course Lemmer had delivered showed a positive perception.[146] Students agreed that

- the course increased their analytical and problem-solving skills;
- the group work helped them understand the practice of law; and
- important lawyering skills were emphasized during the course;
- the professor assisted them to apply theory to solve problems;[147]

Probably most importantly, students showed preference to take another course using the Flipped Classroom model in the future.[148] Similarly, Slomanson when flipping his Civil Procedure course was also able to observe that his students 'wanted more classes to be flipped'.[149]

These conclusions are mirrored by a survey carried out by Beck. Beck replaced some of the traditional lectures with video mini-lectures when teaching International Law at the University of Wisconsin.[150] Students supported the new teaching approach and commented that the online mini-lectures were convenient and improved their comprehension.[151] However, a small group of students complained that the mini-lectures were 'too time-consuming'.[152]

Hess in his paper, summarized Jay Caufield's interviews with graduate 'students who had significant experience in taking blended courses'.[153] Students said the interaction with the faculty was better than in traditional courses.[154] They noticed two major changes in their learning experience, namely taking more responsibility for their learning and reflecting more on the assigned topics before coming to classes.[155] However, students also identified challenges such as technical difficulties and 'the lack of consistency between course websites in various courses'.[156]

McKellar and Maharg incorporated video lectures in the Virtual Learning Environment (VLE) of their Criminal and Civil Procedure courses.[157] Most of the

[146]Lemmer, p. 490.

[147]*Ibid.*

[148]*Ibid.*

[149]Slomanson, p. 100.

[150]Beck, p. 273.

[151]*Ibid*, pp. 278, 282.

[152]*Ibid.*

[153]Hess, pp. 60–61.

[154]*Ibid*, p. 61.

[155]*Ibid*, p. 62.

[156]*Ibid.*

[157]McKellar/Maharg, p. 44.

students responded in a survey that the new VLE has enhanced their learning processes.[158] The videos were flexibly usable enabling them to view the video lectures for revision purposes repeatedly, pause and replay whenever they needed time to reflect or fast forward whenever they were confident about the content.[159] However, some students reported that some teachers being unaware of the schedule of videos covered the same content in class resulting in a lot of repetition.[160] One student reported that since she did not have a computer at home and lived far from the university, she had no access to the videos and the new course design has worked to her disadvantage.[161]

Paechter and Maier carried out a survey on students' preferences for online or face-to-face components.[162] Participating students were chosen with the goal to achieve representative views from a number of universities in Austria.[163] The results show that students' preferences were divided. Online learning components were applauded for

- clarity and explicit structuring of the course and learning contents;
- favourable cost-benefit ratio of effort and learning outcomes;
- fast feedback from the tutor;
- interaction with peer students;
- flexibility of learning with regard to time and place;
- flexibility with regard to about learning strategies and pace of learning.[164]

However, students preferred face-to-face components over online components when it came to the

- counseling and support of learning by the tutor;
- possibility to establish personal contact with the tutor;
- support of cooperative learning and group work with other course participants;
- possibility to establish positive social relations with other course participants;
- support for maintaining learning motivation'.[165]

Students' preference for face-to-face teaching and learning is most apparent in the context of the acquisition of knowledge and skills in scientific work routines, conceptual knowledge in the subject matter, knowledge application and communication

---

[158]*Ibid*, p. 54.
[159]Compare *ibid*, p. 48.
[160]*Ibid*, p. 50.
[161]*Ibid*, p. 55.
[162]Paechter/Maier, p. 292.
[163]*Ibid*.
[164]*Ibid*, p. 295, Table 3 (reformatted, but otherwise reproduced here word for word).
[165]*Ibid*.

and cooperation skills.[166] Only with regard to skills training in self-regulated learning, students prefer online learning components.[167]

3.3.6 Learning Theories

Several academics have tried to explain the rationale behind the Flipped Classroom model by referring to learning theories and cognitive science.[168]

Gerdy et al. have done so in relation to a legal research and writing lecture.[169] They suggest that technology enhancement is beneficial to teaching because it helps educators to accommodate different learning styles and student-centered learning theories.[170] Using Keefe's definition, Gerdy et al. explain learning styles as 'characteristic cognitive, affective, and psychological behaviors that serve as relatively stable indicators of how learners perceive, interact with, and respond to the learning environment.'[171] It is normal that there are students with different learning styles in every classroom. Law teachers should consequently avoid the application of any teaching method across the board.[172] Also, they should try to assess the learning styles of students before incorporating technology into their teaching strategies.[173]

Gerdy's conclusions coincide to some extent with those of Lustbader, Boyle and Dunn. Lustbader suggests that the reason for law students' difficulties in their studies is a disconnection between what their teachers teach and what they learn.[174] Lustbader feels that 'a significant number of law students are not learning or performing at the level of their capabilities' in part because the current method of teaching lacks context.[175] Law students would learn better if they could relate to what they learn which may again differ depending on the students' background.[176] Boyle and Dunn describe the traditional law school pedagogy, the Socratic Method, as a 'group method' rather than an 'individual method'.[177] They argue that the current pedagogy is based on the assumption that all students will learn 'in a

---

166 *Ibid.*

167 *Ibid.*

168 Gerdy/Wise/Craig; Lemmer.

169 Gerdy/Wise/Craig, p. 275.

170 *Ibid*, p. 266.

171 *Ibid.*; also see Le Brun/Johnstone, p. 77, who identify learning styles by a number of educational theories as an important factor to improve students' learning.

172 *Ibid*, pp. 266–267 quoting Lustbader, p. 402.

173 *Ibid*, p. 274.

174 Lustbader, p. 402.

175 *Ibid.*

176 *Ibid*, p. 405.

177 Boyle/Dunn, p. 218.

parallel fashion from any given exchange between student and instructor',[178] without giving consideration to the differences in individual learning styles.[179] They advise educators to use teaching strategies that are congruent with the students' learning styles to generate higher achievement.[180]

Friedman and Alley also note that similar to students with their preferred learning styles, teachers have their preferred teaching styles.[181] 'Teachers need to guard against over-teaching by their own preferred learning styles'.[182] Teachers should help students identify their own learning styles and provide them the opportunity to learn through their preferred styles.[183] However, while students may feel alienated if they are forced to learn in a less preferred style, a number of academics advise against an over-reliance on students' preferred style as this may prevent students from developing skills to adopt to different learning and working environments.[184] Teachers should rather develop specific learning activities to diversify students' learning styles.[185]

Gerdy et al. have also discussed student-centered learning principles and why the use of technology in legal education is beneficial.[186] Student-centered learning principles are developed based on the adult learning theory called 'andragogy' developed by Malcolm Knowles.[187] According to Knowles, student-centered learning has four premises:

- adult learners are self-directed and prefer to make their own learning decisions and not to be treated like children;[188]
- learning occurs best experientially and students learn best when they can relate new experience to their past experience;[189]
- teachers should foster teachable moments, i.e. when students are 'ready to learn';[190]
- for adult students education is problem-centered rather than subject-centered.[191]

Gerdy et al. explain how technology improves the four premises of student-centered learning. First of all, flexibility enhances self-directedness by

[178] *Ibid.* quoting Teich, pp. 167–168.
[179] *Ibid,* p. 219.
[180] *Ibid,* p. 215.
[181] Friedman/Alley, p. 77.
[182] *Ibid.*
[183] *Ibid,* pp. 77–78.
[184] *Ibid,* Gerdy/Wise/Craig, p. 268; Le Brun/Johnstone, p. 82.
[185] Friedman/Alley, p. 78.
[186] Gerdy/Wise/Craig, p. 269.
[187] *Ibid.*
[188] Knowles, p. 85.
[189] *Ibid,* p. 89.
[190] *Ibid,* p. 91.
[191] *Ibid,* p. 93.

allowing students to select the sequence and timing of their learning.[192] Secondly, access to the internet allows students to gather all the examples they need to improve their experiential understanding of the 'big picture'.[193] Thirdly, technology enables students to prepare outside classrooms, having access to supplemental materials online whenever they feel 'ready'.[194] Finally, Gerdy et al. interpret the last premise as the requirement to integrate a 'real-world' touch to the learning materials.[195] The pedagogy of their legal research and writing course was built precisely on the philosophy that 'students must solve problems and act as practicing lawyers would. The use of technology in so doing is merely an added component of the "reality".'[196]

Gerdy et al.'s opinion on 'readiness-to-learn' corresponds with the 2007 survey results of Larcombe et al. which also reveal that the level of 'readiness-to-learn' appears to have a positive effect on students' academic results.[197] The (self-rating) survey was collected from LLB students studying at the University of Melbourne Law School.[198] In an effort to identify factors that appear to affect law students' first semester academic performance, academic 'readiness' was identified together with two other factors, namely 'interest in the content and tasks involved in studying law' and 'a realistic understanding of the workload'.[199] The self-rating of academic 'readiness' reveals that there was an obvious gap between subgroups of students.[200] High-achieving students on average rated their readiness higher than low-achieving students.[201] The results imply that high-achieving students were the least likely to anticipate academic difficulties and 'would take a more conscientious approach to their learning than low-achieving students'.[202] The results highlight the importance of 'readiness-to-learn' as a factor to improve learning outcomes.

The video lectures used by Gerdy et al. in a trial-run led them to conclude that legal research videos were among the most successful of their learning activities.[203] The videos were well-received by students.[204] Students enjoyed the implied flexibility which allowed them to watch the video lectures on their own terms and

---

[192]Gerdy/Wise/Craig, p. 269.
[193]*Ibid*, p. 270.
[194]*Ibid.*
[195]*Ibid*, p. 271.
[196]*Ibid.*
[197]Larcombe/Nichloson/Malkin, p. 96.
[198]*Ibid*, pp. 96, 105.
[199]*Ibid*, p. 96.
[200]*Ibid*, Table 3, p. 117.
[201]*Ibid*, pp. 116–117.
[202]*Ibid*, pp. 117–118.
[203]Gerdy/Wise/Craig, p. 289.
[204]*Ibid*, p. 288.

review the materials whenever they needed to.[205] The use of video lectures did not diminish the quality of content delivery. When comparing the exam results of blended course models with traditional lectures, there was no measurable difference in scores.[206]

Lemmer on the other hand used the 'informed learning theory' to justify the flipping of a Legal Research class.[207] She explains that it was the objective of the course to enable students to reach a level of information literacy so that they know how to access and engage in any information in their legal career.[208] Lemmer quotes Bruce et al. to explain informed learning as 'learning through engaging with or interacting with information'[209] and for informed learning to be effective, it should be 'learner-centered, experiential and reflective'.[210] Thus, it is the responsibility of law teachers to develop a curriculum that supports informed learning to help students cultivate the required legal information literacy.[211]

Lemmer points out that traditional legal research courses had oversimplified the process of research to a linear model.[212] Traditionally, legal research was taught in the print environment, with focus on searching skills of relevant case reports, primary and secondary legal sources.[213] Students are denied the opportunities to experience and engage with information in a more dynamic way which is nowadays often required by the legal profession.[214] Lemmer's Flipped Classroom model was designed to tackle the inadequacy of the traditional course design by providing a supportive environment that enables students to develop the information literacy.[215] After viewing the instructional materials, students were to come to lab sessions ready to work on research hypotheticals in small groups.[216] The hypotheticals often required students to advise a client, modeling a law office, to train students to think and interact like lawyers.[217] Student feedback in relation to the redesigned Legal Research course was positive.[218] The overall professional and academic gains achieved by students confirmed that flipping the classroom was successful.[219]

---

[205] *Ibid.*

[206] *Ibid*, p. 289.

[207] Lemmer, p. 474.

[208] *Ibid*, p. 479.

[209] *Ibid*, p. 475.

[210] *Ibid*, quoting Diekema/Holliday/Leary, p. 261.

[211] Compare *ibid*, p. 477.

[212] *Ibid*, p. 476 with reference to Diekema/Holliday/Leary, p. 261.

[213] *Ibid*, p. 475.

[214] *Ibid*, p. 476, quoting Diekema/Holliday/Leary, p. 261.

[215] *Ibid*, p. 481.

[216] *Ibid*, pp. 473, 482.

[217] *Ibid*, pp. 473, 481.

[218] *Ibid*, p. 490.

[219] *Ibid*, p. 491.

3.3.7 Learning Needs

Academics suggest that Flipped Classrooms can accommodate various learning needs.[220] Learning needs can be multidimensional. In her study of the 21st century law students in the U.K., Bone found that nowadays there is a high percentage (47 %) of working students.[221] The survey reveals that despite the increase of working students over the past decade, little has changed in teaching styles to accommodate these students' learning needs.[222] A study conducted by Macdonald shows that there is an increasing demand for blended learning among mature students.[223] In particular, mature students often appreciate the flexibility blended learning can offer.[224]

Polding points out that there is a diversity of learning needs, such as for students with dyslexia and students with English as a second language.[225] The different needs should be taken into account when designing course structures and contents. Polding reveals that when asked how they would like to participate in Flipped Classrooms, 'students with English as a second language and students with family commitments were particularly positive'. However, students question whether a webcast is adequate as the replacement of traditional classroom teaching.[226]

Le Brun and Johnstone emphasize the importance for teachers to appreciate the difference in learning needs arising out of cultural differences.[227] Lemmer explains that the social and cultural background of international LLM students requires them to adjust to the U.S. system and to overcome cultural barriers.[228] She explains that the Flipped Classroom setting can cater to the learning needs of foreign students in that Flipped Classrooms encourage students to experiment, challenge, and gain a deeper understanding of the U.S. legal system.[229] In turn this provides them the confidence 'to engage in legal practice in the United States and elsewhere'.[230]

---

220 Compare Lemmer; Macdonald; Polding.

221 Bone, p. 229.

222 *Ibid*, p. 231

223 Macdonald, p. 33.

224 *Ibid.*

225 Polding, p. 3.

226 *Ibid*, p. 6.

227 Le Brun/Johnstone, p. 69.

228 Lemmer, p. 467.

229 *Ibid*, p. 468.

230 *Ibid.*

3.3.8 Bloom's Taxonomy

Lihosit and Larrington use Bloom's taxonomy to explain the reason why flipping their Advanced Legal Research classroom was beneficial. They argue that it allowed higher-order learning activities to take place inside the classroom.[231] According to Bloom's taxonomy there are six levels of learning activities. Lower-order activities are knowledge acquisition and comprehension.[232] In contrast, application, analysis, synthesis and evaluation qualify as higher-order learning activities.[233] In a traditional classroom, where teachers merely have enough time to focus on the conveyance of information, only lower-order learning activities can be conducted.[234] Higher-order learning activities would be the preparation of homework or conducting online tutorials, writing legal memoranda, or assigned research work.[235] In a traditional classroom setting not many students attempt to engage in higher-order learning activities and the overall learning outcome is low.[236] By contrast, in Flipped Classrooms the lower-order learning activities happen outside of classroom when students view the video lectures.[237] The freed-up classroom time allows teachers to engage in higher-order learning.[238] Higher-order learning activities are of particular importance for law classrooms as they enable students to foster critical thinking skills and practice the skills they acquired through viewing the videos.[239]

3.3.9 The Debate Regarding the Use of Technology

The benefits of using technology in legal education are widely acknowledged. Nevertheless, academics are cautious when embracing technology.[240] Legal academics may be concerned that the use of technology would oversimplify the classroom experience or diminish the integrity of legal education.[241] As an example of how counterproductive technology can be, Caron and Gely point out that the over-reliance on PowerPoints has led to passivity in learning.[242]

---

[231]Lihosit/Larrington, p. 4.

[232]*Ibid*, pp. 1, 3.

[233]*Ibid.*

[234]*Ibid*, p. 3.

[235]*Ibid.*

[236]*Ibid.*

[237]*Ibid*, p. 4.

[238]*Ibid.*

[239]*Ibid.*

[240]Compare *supra*, 1.2.2.

[241]Compare Galves, p. 234; Binford, p. 167.

[242]Caron/Gely, pp. 551, 556, quoting Leslie, pp. 1304–1306.

Galves, however, argues that often it is not the use of technology, but rather bad pedagogy which creates an undesirable learning environment.[243] Technology can be counterproductive only when teachers are oversimplifying teaching in the first place.[244] An effective interaction between teachers and students requires teachers to master communication skills and perceive technology as enhancement to teaching rather than a threat.[245] Lemmer agrees in that technology should only be used when it supports learning objectives and outcomes.[246] Teaching strategies must be designed carefully to ensure that they drive the use of technology and not vice versa.[247]

Maharg explains the reason why law teachers see technologies as a threat. The introduction of instant communication technology is 'a new twist to an old thread of protest, where teachers perceive they are oppressed in one way or another by varied forms of new educational practice.'[248] But as the society calls for a change in the culture and role of teachers, it is time to move forward and technology does not have to be disempowering and can improve teaching if the faculty is willing to take one step at a time.[249]

Nehme advises law teachers to take into account the technological ability of students and beware of computer anxiety when adopting e-learning tools.[250] Academics also report that students may encounter technical difficulties.[251] In extreme cases, students may not even have access to computers at all.[252] Teachers need to be complacent about students' IT skills before embracing technology and never underestimate computer anxiety.[253] Computer anxiety may lower students' motivation to learn. 'This may be especially true of first-year law students.'[254] Facing the transition from school to university, first-year students may not be comfortable with technology-enhanced learning.[255] If students lack computer or internet skills necessary for the Flipped Classroom learning, technology would only build up their stress level during the transition.[256]

---

[243]Galves, p. 234.

[244]*Ibid*, p. 235.

[245]*Ibid*, pp. 197–198.

[246]Lemmer, p. 466.

[247]Compare Hess, p. 79.

[248]Maharg, under 'Teaching Staff and ICT'.

[249]Compare *ibid.* under 'Changing Cultures of Use and Identity'.

[250]Nehme, p. 229.

[251]Hess, p. 62; Ireland, p. 157; Macdonald, p. 37.

[252]McKellar/Maharg, p. 55; compare *supra*, 3.3.5.

[253]Nehme, p. 230.

[254]*Ibid.*

[255]*Ibid.*

[256]*Ibid.*

Ireland cautions that it cannot be assumed that technology improves the teaching and learning environment just because students are 'digital natives'.[257] Digital native students may have different learning styles and may not always be comfortable with technology.[258] In fact, an empirical study on the effect of podcasts on students' learning shows that not all students prefer the use of this study technique.[259] Those who prefer face-to-face lecturing explain that they could concentrate better and absorb more in a traditional lecture.[260] Extra attention should be paid if there are mature students in the classroom as their computer skills may be much less advanced.[261] MacDonald agrees that mature students may feel anxieties due to a lack of IT skills and access to computers and may need additional support.[262] To address potential technical challenges face-to-face sessions may be held to clarify some technical issues in mid-term or provided technical assistance by telephone.[263]

3.3.10 Issues with 'Flipping'

Jones asks whether video lectures can deliver the benefits of a face-to-face lecture effectively.[264] Traditionally, the physical presence of both teachers and students has been an essential component of any lecture.[265] Teachers may keep students actively involved through the lecture by encouraging them to listen and respond to the content.[266] In face-to-face settings teachers can observe students' reaction and thus assess the level of understanding so that teachers may vary the amount and speed of lecturing and provide instant feedback to students.[267] The presence of teachers may not only be necessary for the delivery of lecture contents. In contrast, the physical appearance of a teacher itself can be important for encouraging students to learn. If the value of lecturing lies in the physical presence of teachers as Jones suggests, then any virtual presence during flipped lectures may not be as effective.[268] Jones believes that teaching presence can be achieved as long as the online course design encourages a faculty-student interaction, a learning community exists and students

---

257 Ireland, p. 157.

258 *Ibid.*

259 Kazlauska/Robinson, p. 328.

260 *Ibid.*

261 Ireland, p. 157.

262 MacDonald, p. 37.

263 *Ibid*, p. 39.

264 Jones, p. 77.

265 *Ibid*, p. 76.

266 *Ibid.*

267 *Ibid.*

268 *Ibid*, p. 77.

are engaged with the course material.[269] In fact, the Flipped Classroom concept does not do away with in-class face-to-face teaching, i.e virtual lectures do not diminish in-class face-to-face interaction between students and teachers. The online lectures are rather added to in-class sessions which, however, now allow for more interactivity. In other words, Flipped Classrooms change the in-class teaching to a more interactive mode and add online lectures.

3.4 Socratic Method Versus Flipped Classrooms

3.4.1 General

In particular North American law schools have long promoted and used the so-called Socratic Method for teaching purposes. On first sight, the Socratic Method is based on the same idea like Flipped Classrooms, i.e to use pre-class or outside-class learning activities to transfer knowledge to students to free time for in-class interactivity.

The following sections first introduce the Socratic Method, then report on studies conducted in relation to the Socratic Method and finally compare the Socratic Method with the Flipped Classroom concept.

3.4.2 What Is the Socratic Method?

The Socratic Method has been used for over 100 years in North American law schools.[270] It is still the predominant model used in legal education in the U.S. In fact, the 'Socratic Method has long been considered a defining element of American legal education'.[271] In contrast, the lecture mode seems to be more popular in law schools in the U.K. and Australia and also in Europe.[272]

The Socratic Method was introduced to American law schools in 1870s by Christopher Langdell, the then Dean of Harvard Law School.[273] The method's basic idea is rather simple: in class a law teacher randomly calls on students' names and questions their understanding of the day's pre-class reading assignments.[274] The Socratic Method is sometimes also called the 'case method' because the

---

[269]*Ibid*, p. 99.

[270]Donahoe, p. 487.

[271]Kerr, p. 113.

[272]Compare *supra*, 3.2.3.

[273]Donahoe, p. 487; Schneider, pp. 27–28.

[274]Donahoe, *ibid*; The Carnegie Report, pp. 48–49.

Socratic dialogue is often on case law.[275] It encourages discussions around casebooks which contain appellate court cases.[276] The in-class Q&A sessions usually involve the stating of facts of cases, the identification of applicable legal rules and the application of concepts to hypothetical situations.[277] Some teachers stay for the discussion of particular questions with one student, others move to other students frequently.[278] Langdell anticipated that this student-centered conversation encourages deeper thinking, analyzing and critiquing of legal principles which in turn cultivates the legal expertise required by the profession.[279] In the last thirty years, the interpretation of the Socratic Method has seen a significant process of transformation.[280] The traditional question-and-answer remains the norm, but the new interpretation includes 'toned-down Socratic questioning, student panels, group discussions, and lectures'.[281]

3.4.3 How Does the Socratic Method Work?

According to Langdell, the Socratic Method is an effective pedagogy because it promotes critical thinking and improves the analytical skills of law students. It requires an examination of assumptions and discovery of mistakes and correction or refinement of the assumption.[282] The Socratic Method involves a back and forth dialogue between two people and consists of five stages.[283]

- Stage one: wonder—a question is posed.
- Stage two: hypothesis—the question is followed by a hypothetical answer.
- Stage three: elenchus (refutation and cross-examination)—the answer is tested and cross-checked for its values.
- Stage four: acceptance/rejection of the hypothesis—the hypothesis is accepted as provisionally true and a return to stage three is required if there are other predictable consequences of the answer which have not been confirmed yet.
- Stage five: action.[284]

---

[275] *Ibid.*; see, however, Stropus, pp. 453–454, clarifying the difference between Langdell's case method and the Socratic Method.

[276] Compare Fitzgerald, p. 60.

[277] Caron/Gely, p. 554.

[278] *Ibid*;.

[279] Compare Carnegie Report, p. 11; Donahoe, p. 487; Schneider, p. 28.

[280] Kerr, p. 114.

[281] *Ibid.*

[282] Compare Stropus, pp. 468–69.

[283] Boghossian 2012, p. 711.

[284] *Ibid*, pp. 711–712.

The advantages of the Socratic Method are seen in the following points:

The Socratic Method requires students to challenge their own assumptions repeatedly thus developing their analytical skills. 'By posing questions to students that force them to confront the weaknesses of each position, the Socratic professor ultimately trains students to assess the strength of legal arguments on their own'.[285] With the repeated training process eventually internalized, the students will become independent thinkers and more sophisticated in understanding the law.[286] The Socratic Method teaches students to be self-responsible towards their study 'by teaching them how to teach themselves'.[287] It also allows students to appreciate the complexity of the law and instill a sense of skepticism about the law.[288] The Socratic dialogue also enhances interactions in the classroom. With students constantly questioning presumptions made by their peers and engaging in debates the classroom will become lively and students are motivated to prepare for classes.[289] By speaking in class regularly, students are building up their communication and advocacy skills, which is essential for the legal profession.[290]

But, does the Socratic Method in practice really deliver these alleged outcomes? When looking for answers in the existing legal education literature, one will find that surprisingly little empirical data have been gathered on the effectiveness of the Socratic Method.[291] In contrast, the question whether the Socratic Method produces 'better' academic results in terms of students' learning experience and learning outcomes is predominantly discussed based on anecdotal evidence and observations.

In the next sections, we report in more detail on the arguments in favour and against the Socratic Method as put forward by the legal educational literature. We regard these arguments as important for the purposes of this book as they may in the same way be valid also in relation to the Flipped Classroom concept. In other words, the discussion of the Socratic Method may inform the understanding of the viability of Flipped Classrooms.

3.4.4 Active Learning Principle

One of the core arguments in favor of the Socratic Method is that it improves teaching and learning (compared with the lecture mode) by providing 'a more "active" learning environment'.[292]

---

[285]Kerr, p. 117.

[286]*Ibid.*

[287]Garner, pp. 1605–1606.

[288]*Ibid*, p. 1606.

[289]Kerr, p. 117.

[290]*Ibid.*; Korn, p. 588.

[291]Compare in general Fitzgerald, pp. 63–64; Laster, p. 264.

[292]Garner, p. 1605.

Active learning is understood as producing lasting values and equipping students with the ability to process new information as well as with problem-solving skills.[293] To achieve these goals 'students should be engaged in behavior and activities other than listening'.[294] If students are put at the receiving end of an information transfer the active learning process is very limited.[295] And, this is unlike requiring students to talk, write, read or reflect.[296] Both talking and writing require students to clarify their thoughts based on what they have 'heard, read, observed or experienced'.[297] Reading and reflecting are seen as critical components of active learning because students are forced to engage in clarifying information conveyed by others.[298] At first glance, the Socratic Method seems to meet all the requirements of the active learning principle. In fact, constant reflection stands in its center.[299] The Socratic Method has, however, also faced criticism.

3.4.5 Arguments Contra the Socratic Method

3.4.5.1 General

According to Schwartz the Socratic Method scores poorly on two accounts, namely vicarious learning and self-teaching.[300] Since the Socratic conversation takes place as a one-on-one interaction between the teacher and one student, the rest of the class is merely listening, resulting in passive learning on their part.[301] Except for the student who is actually questioned by the teacher, the rest of the class learns by watching the interaction without participating in the dialogue.[302] From this viewpoint the Socratic Method may not implement the active learning principle appropriately.

The second issue with the Socratic Method is that it entails that students are self-teaching. However, students may not be able to remain on top of a constantly deepening Socratic dialogue without the help of the teacher.[303] Some of the skills students are required to develop are: factual understanding, legal analysis, legal

[293]Caron/Gely, pp. 552–553.

[294]*Ibid*, p. 552.

[295]*Ibid*; contrast this with the lecture mode, see *supra,* 3.2.2.

[296]Caron/Gely, p. 553.

[297]*Ibid.*

[298]*Ibid.*

[299]*Ibid*, p. 554.

[300]Schwartz, p. 357.

[301]*Ibid.* p. 351; Caron/Gely, p. 554.

[302]Caron/Gely, *ibid.*

[303]Compare Schwarz, p. 352.

reasoning, issue spotting and drafting.[304] Not every student picks up these skills quickly enough and often students are left confused without the law teacher pointing to the right direction. Schwartz compares the first year law classroom to a hypothetical swimming class. The Socratic Method is equivalent to a situation where somebody attempts to learn swimming by merely watching their classmate's demonstration without the teachers giving any instruction.[305] The swimming class is doomed to fail on the basis of being ineffective, inefficient and unappealing.[306]

3.4.5.2 The Socratic Method Does Not Teach Practical Skills

The most recent evaluation of the Socratic Method is probably the Carnegie Report '*Educating Lawyers*'.[307] The Carnegie Report concludes that the Socratic Method over-emphasizes the importance of cases and lacks focus on clients.[308]

As a matter of fact, the criticism that law schools' do not offer sufficient practical training can be traced back to the 1930s.[309] Jerome Frank, an early critics on the Langellian case-method criticized the Socratic classroom as 'an overly academic and library focused product of Langdellian legal science'.[310] In Frank's view, the mere teaching of the 'library law' may produce law graduates competent in abstract legal-reasoning but without practical lawyering skills.[311]

According to Blasi the most valued qualities of lawyers are 'oral communication', 'written communication' and 'instilling others' confidence in you'.[312] The most important skills or areas of knowledge are 'ability in legal analysis and legal reasoning, drafting legal documents and ability to diagnose and plan solutions for legal problems'.[313] Frank points out that the Socratic Method exceedingly concentrates on the studying of precedents leading to an oversimplification which neglects the need for students to understand how courts arrive at their decisions.

[304]*Ibid.*

[305]*Ibid*, pp. 354–355.

[306]*Ibid.*

[307]Compare *supra*, 1.2.1. The Carnegie Report is one of a series of reports on professional education issued by the Carnegie Foundation for the Advancement of Teaching prepared by William M. Sullivan, Anne Colby, Judith Welch Wegner, Lloyd Bond and Lee S. Shulman The Report summarizes the findings of studies on how law schools develop legal understanding and professional identity. Over the academic year 1999–2000, the research team visited 16 law schools in the United States and Canada for this purpose, p. 15.

[308]*Ibid*, pp. 56–57.

[309]Compare Kerr, p. 119, footnote 26.

[310]Kerr, *ibid.*

[311]Frank, p. 908.

[312]Blasi, p. 326.

[313]*Ibid.*

Confining the attention of teaching of *stare decisis*, law school teaching has oversimplified the practice of law.[314]

3.4.5.3 The Socratic Method Is Unexciting and Cannot Convey Large Amounts of Information

According to Garner, the Socratic Method is only 'exciting' in the first year of law school.[315] After the first year, most of the students can no longer appreciate the method and become bored.[316] Second, as the conversation often focuses on a few students, the remaining students are passive listeners. Since cross-examination occupies 99 % of the time, only 1 % of the class-time remains for the correct answer.[317] Garner concludes that the reliance on vicarious learning is not effective.[318] And, the Socratic method does not appear to be the most suitable way to instill students with large amounts of information.[319] Because of the limitation of class time, the level of coverage is compromised with questions unanswered, resulting in confusion on the students' part.[320]

3.4.5.4 The Socratic Method Fosters Monopolization by 'a Vocal Few'

Garner also reports that the Socratic Method is sometimes regarded as degrading and demeaning students and in turn discouraging participation.[321] It 'fosters monopolization by a vocal few' and forces students who dislike this teaching mode to go along anyway.[322] Finally, the Socratic Method may reinforce discrimination issues, e.g in relation to minority and female students.[323]

3.4.5.5 The Socratic Method Causes Distress Among Students

The Socratic Method is often criticized for causing distress among students.[324] 'One empirical report estimated that up to 40 % of law students may experience

---

314 Frank, pp. 912–913.

315 Garner, p. 1609.

316 *Ibid.*

317 *Ibid*, pp. 1609–1610.

318 *Ibid.*

319 *Ibid*, p. 1610.

320 Compare *ibid* ,p. 1611.

321 *Ibid.*

322 *Ibid.*

323 *Ibid*, 1614, 1617; 1625; also see Kerr, pp. 118–119; Roach, pp. 675–677; Stropus, pp. 462–463.

324 Donahoe, p. 487; Gottfredson/Panter/Daye/Allen/Wightman/Deo, p. 520; Kerr, p. 118; Stropus, pp. 456–457.

depression or other symptoms.'[325] Many students find the teacher-controlled approach unappealing. Students often felt humiliated and degraded because the Socratic teachers are 'quick to criticize imperfect student answers'.[326]

Roach has observed that the reasons for causing law students' distress are plenty, with the use of the Socratic Method being one of them.[327] Roach argues that the more compelling explanation is 'the lack of context'.[328] Students are isolated not only from their peers or faculty, but also pedagogically.[329] They are given little instruction on how to study and what is expected of them.[330] The Socratic dialogue leaves them with little guidance in terms of substance and where and how to seek help, leading to great distress.[331] Roach has warned that the problem of isolation seems to be more pervasive for minority race and other non-traditional law students, affecting their academic results eventually.[332]

Kerr explains that non-traditional students such as women and minorities are less in favor of the Socratic Method because 'they are likely to be used as "spokespersons" for their race or gender' against the backdrop of having experienced discrimination already in other contexts.[333] Stropus suggests that non-traditional law students often 'experience an added sense of alienation' which in turn hurts their motivation towards studying thus affecting their academic results.[334] According to Stropus 'twenty-five percent of the females and twenty-two percent of the minority females experienced a loss of confidence because of the classroom experience. In contrast, only fifteen percent of the males reported experiencing a loss of confidence.'[335]

Garner agrees that female students often find the Socratic Method intimidating.[336] He highlights one survey done by the University of Pennsylvania, reporting that many women feel being put on the spot when asked to answer a question.[337] The required 'performance' added pressure for female students thus undermining their learning experience.[338] Garner concludes that women find the adversarial law

---

[325] Roach, p. 670, quoting Benjamin pp. 246–247.

[326] Kerr, p. 118.

[327] Roach, p. 671. Other reasons are the workload, the total absence of feedback and an 'unsupportive' law school environment.

[328] *Ibid*, p. 672.

[329] *Ibid.*

[330] *Ibid.*

[331] *Ibid*, p. 672.

[332] *Ibid*, pp. 675–677.

[333] Kerr, p. 118; Garner, p. 1623.

[334] Stropus, p. 462.

[335] *Ibid*, pp. 462–463.

[336] Garner, p. 1623.

[337] *Ibid.*

[338] *Ibid.*

school environment intimidating and 'its emphasis on abstract as opposed to contextual reasoning to be unappealing and disengaging'.[339]

3.4.6 Students' Feedback

Fitzgerald conducted an empirical research on the educational practices at a Canadian university. In-depth interviews were carried out with 19 law graduates who had completed their LL.B. programme earlier.[340] The survey focused on

- the educational practices the students experienced in their first year law school, and
- their perception on the impact of these practices.[341]

The survey implies that most students preferred for the lecture method as opposed to the Socratic Method. Almost all students agreed that the lecture method was an effective way to convey information.[342] Only one graduate complained that the lecture method lacks interaction and described the teacher was 'reciting rather than communicating or engaging',[343] causing some students to 'zone out' in lectures.[344] One reason for students' preference for the lecture method was the amount of materials to be covered by law students and the difficulty in reading cases which was regarded as difficult without the guidance offered in a lecture.[345] Most students consequently relied on lectures to find out what was important.[346] It was also for this reason that they did not like the Socratic Method. They resented having to prepare for classes and felt intimidated and uncomfortable being put on the spot and called upon in front of their peers.[347] Most students did not appreciate answers from other students.[348] One student felt that the purpose of Q&A sessions was to check up or intimidate students, rather than to encourage creative thinking.[349] Only a few students said they appreciated the questions because they encouraged students to come prepared for class. But still, they still commented that the whole process led to

[339]*Ibid*, p. 1624.

[340]Fitzgerald, p. 60.

[341]*Ibid*, p. 64.

[342]*Ibid*, p. 83 and *passim*.

[343]*Ibid*, p. 68.

[344]*Ibid.*

[345]*Ibid*, p. 66.

[346]*Ibid.*

[347]*Ibid*, p. 67.

[348]*Ibid.*

[349]*Ibid*, p. 68.

too much stress.[350] Most students said they could have benefited from more guidance and more feedback from the teachers.[351]

3.4.7 Defending the Socratic Method

Despite the criticism, the Socratic Method still receives broad support. Bognossian argues that it is the ultimate goal of the Socratic Method to help students to see the mistake in their own argument so they can correct them.[352] As long as the discussion centers around the argument, the issue of race and gender will not play a role in the Socratic dialogue. 'The elenchus does not necessarily bring one's racial and gender assumptions to the surface, but it does force the participants to focus on the arguments and not the people who make the arguments.'[353] Boghossian argues that it is therefore incorrect to accuse the Socratic Method of discrimination against race and gender.[354] Problems may rather be a result of misapplication of the Socratic Method by teachers who believe that humiliation helps students to learn thus abusing their power through the Socratic Method.[355]

Laster defends the Socratic Method and submits that students who complain about the Socratic Method being stressful must remember that stress is an inevitable part of lawyering and it is the job of their teachers to prepare students for professional work.[356] The Socratic dialogue is merely the training for entering into a career where stress is expected.[357] Laster suggests that the training offered by the Socratic Method may have a direct relationship to the success in professional life.[358] It remains unclear why some students handle stress better than others. However, it is certain that the ability to cope with stress is critical in studying law and a successful legal career.[359] Some students participate actively in a Socratic classroom but others do not. They all have their own reasons whether to speak up in class or remain in silence. But, law students should be mature enough to make their own choice in relation to their preferred and most suitable learning strategy.[360]

---

[350] *Ibid*, p. 68.

[351] *Ibid*, p. 70.

[352] Boghossian 2012, p. 713.

[353] Boghossian 2002, p. 3.

[354] *Ibid.*

[355] Boghossian 2002, pp. 3–4; Boghossian 2012, p. 714.

[356] Laster, pp. 268–269.

[357] *Ibid.*; compare Carrington, p. 461.

[358] Laster, *ibid.*

[359] *Ibid.*

[360] Compare *ibid*, p. 268.

Laster warns against putting too much weight on the personal experiences of students.[361] The emphasis on student experience and the consumerist agenda that regards students as the consumers to be serviced by universities may create an illusion that learning has to be pleasant to be effective.[362] It may be a misperception that effective pedagogy must always cater to students' personal experience and preferences. In fact, the value of any pedagogy should not be lost in 'a popularity contest'. Students may not 'like' a particular way of teaching yet discover it to be useful once they enter into the profession.[363]

3.4.8 Variations of the Socratic Method

The criticism of the Socratic Method did not go unnoticed and perhaps for this reason, by the mid-20th century, the Socratic Method has seen variations as compared with its original form.[364] But it was not until the 1950s–1960s that the Socratic Method was replaced by fine-tuned approaches as already mentioned above.[365]

3.4.9 Comparing the Socratic Method and the Flipped Classroom Concept

The previous sections have introduced the Socratic Method and arguments put forward in support and against it. This was done based on the understanding that the Socratic Method and the Flipped Classroom are founded on a similar rationale.

In fact, it is the main idea of the Socratic Method and also of the Flipped Classroom concept that the (pure) lecture mode may be insufficient to achieve desired learning outcomes and that in-class interactivity should be improved. However, while the Socratic Method—at least in its original form—attempts to do away with lectures altogether—the Flipped Classroom concept does not. The Flipped Classroom concept rather aims to replace in-class lectures with online

---

[361]*Ibid*, p. 263.

[362]Broadbent/Sellman pp. 46, 53.

[363]Laster, p. 263.

[364]Schneider, p. 29.

[365]*Supra*, 3.4.2; compare Kerr, p. 114. Kerr interviewed 12 professors teaching in Harvard Law School on their teaching styles and their views on the Socratic Method. He found that five were best described as traditionalists, three as quasi-traditionalist and four as counter-traditionalists, each group using the Socratic method in different ways, *Ibid*, p. 122. It is notable that regardless of their teaching styles, professors of all three categories adopted lecture modules to a certain extent.

lectures. Some of the criticism of the Socratic Method related to difficulties in information transfer does therefore not necessarily apply to the use of Flipped Classrooms.

Another major difference between the Socratic Method and the Flipped Classroom concept is that the Socratic Method focuses on the question how in-class time is to be filled, i.e with lectures or a Socratic discourse. In contrast, the Flipped Classroom concept is not at all concerned with the form of in-class interactivity and does in this regard not limit itself. The discussion surrounding the Flipped Classroom concept rather focuses on how lectures can be made available online to free in-class time for interactivity. Some academics[366] have recommended combining Flipped Classrooms with the Socratic Method by asking students to watch pre-recorded videos and later engage them in an in-class Socratic dialogue.

The Socratic Method and the Flipped Classroom concept consequently differ in relation to the way how the in-class lecture should be replaced with out-of-classroom learning activities. Despite some variations in more recent times, the Socratic Method traditionally relies on reading assignments to replace lectures.[367] This is not surprising given that the Socratic Method was developed long ago when online resources were not available. The Flipped Classroom concept focuses instead on out-of-classroom online lectures and much discussion surrounds the question if and how online lectures can be and should be developed.[368]

Considering these fundamentally different *foci* of the Socratic Method on the one hand and the Flipped Classroom concept on the other hand it must be concluded that the studies conducted in relation to the Socratic Method can inform the analysis of the viability of the Flipped Classroom concept for legal educational purposes only to a limited extent. This is in relation to the question if and how the lecture mode is suitable for law teaching and learning purposes. Research on the Socratic Method can, however, not contribute to the main point of discussion related to Flipped Classrooms, i.e the advantages and disadvantages of online lectures. Interestingly, in the discussion of Flipped Classrooms it seems to have been taken for granted that in-class interactivity is necessary to achieve good learning outcomes.

Finally, it must be acknowledged that the Socratic Method has been developed specifically for law teaching purposes. In contrast, the Flipped Classroom concept does not have any discipline specific focus. Having said that, it is obvious that the idea underscoring the Socratic Method could be and is probably used in variations in other subject areas as well although related initiatives have not reached the level of conceptualization and sophistication as in the area of law.

---

[366]Ryan/Xin/Yuan/You/Li, p. 348; compare Abrams, p. 567.

[367]Garner, p. 1605: the Socratic Method was introduced to compensate for the inadequacies of textbooks and lecturing.

[368]Compare for a detailed discussion *infra*, 3.5 and 4.

3.5 Video Flipping Versus Audio Flipping

3.5.1 General

Flipped Classrooms can be delivered by either video or audio means[369] and the same is true for any blended teaching method.[370] However, our literature review reveals that the majority of academics use the video mode with only a few have opted to use audio as the media for delivering lectures.[371] In this section, we review the advantages and disadvantages between the two media and the rationale of choices made by academics in their Flipped Classroom models.

3.5.2 Arguments in Favor of the Video Approach

According to Upchurch, there are two main ways to produce videos—the 'white board approach' and the 'screen capture approach'.[372] 'Under the white board approach, the professor simply tapes him- or herself in front of a white board or flip chart. Under the screen capture approach, the professor creates visual presentations, such as PowerPoint or Word documents, and then records her voice while running the presentation on the computer. The video will show the movement on the screen synced with the audio recording.'[373] After production, videos produced in either way have to be uploaded to an internet platform for sharing with students.[374] For the purpose of flipping her course Upchurch chose the 'screen capture approach'.[375]

Despite the fact that the majority of law teacher choose video (either the form of the 'white board approach' or 'screen capture approach') over audio to be the media for content delivery, little is known on why they made this choice.[376] One reason may be the perceived psychological value of the teacher's social (visual) presence at least in the white board approach. One of the students in McKellar and Maharg's case study noted that though she hardly ever looked at the video screen, she acknowledged its importance to her.[377]

---

[369]Compare CADQ, p. 1; Educause, p. 1.

[370]Means/Toyama/Murphy/Bakia/Jones, p. 17.

[371]Academics who use video as the means to deliver content are Beck; Davis/Neary/Vaughn; Gerdy/Wise/Craig; Lemmer; Lihosit/Larrington; McKellar/Maharg; Slomanson; Upchurch; Wood.

[372]Upchurch, p. 3; compare Deakin Learning Futures Teaching Development Team, p. 14.

[373]Upchurch, *ibid.*

[374]*Ibid*, p. 4.

[375]*Ibid*, p. 1.

[376]Compare Beck; Davis/Neary/Vaughn; Gerdy/Wise/Craig; Lemmer; Lihosit/Larrington; McKellar/Maharg; Slomanson; Wood; Upchurch; for the choice made in the context of this study see *infra*, 6.4.3.

[377]McKellar/Maharg, p. 53.

Owston et al. (2011) have questioned the importance of the teacher's social presence.[378] Their case study on how lecture capture affects students' perception and academic outcomes suggests the opposite.[379] Students do not indicate any preference for the presence of teacher shown in the video over the audio approach.[380]

Dey et al. have conducted an empirical study on the learning outcomes and personal effects of providing the images of teachers in a video capture. Their findings show that though students may prefer to view the image of teachers on a video screen, there is no linkage between the viewing and the retention or transfer of knowledge.[381]

The main downside of the white board approach, however, is that it is less sustainable than the 'screen capture' and the audio approach.[382] When an update of even a small part of the lecture content is necessary, the entire video made in the form of the white board approach would have to undergo re-recording. Unless the teacher retains the exact appearance as in the original video, the entire video would feature the same teacher in different outfits, risking the video 'turning into a fashion show'.[383] This could degrade the image of the teacher and the whole course.[384]

The advantage of the screen capture approach is that it can play a PowerPoint slide show and audio recording simultaneously, satisfying learning styles of both visual and auditory learners. In addition, updating a certain part of the lecture content would be relatively easy as only changes to the slide show and re-recording of particular parts are necessary. For our own case study we have adopted the screen capture approach and we are reporting on the reasons for our choice and related practical consequences in a later chapter.[385]

3.5.3 Arguments in Favor of the Audio Approach

The benefits of the audio approach are seen in the fact that modern students prefer multitasking.[386] Listening to audio files allows them to access the lecture while

[378]Owston/Lupshenyuk/Wideman, p. 262.

[379]*Ibid*, p. 266.

[380]*Ibid.*

[381]Dey/Burn/Gerdes, pp. 385–386, 390.

[382]Yeh recommends using the white board approach since it provides a personal touch even though it may require more efforts when content update is necessary. Yeh, Benson, 'How to flip the classroom well—BTS Flipping'. Seminar at the Chinese University of Hong Kong on 24 October 2014.

[383]Yeh also emphasises the importance of wearing the same outfits so as to provide a more consistent and professional perception.

[384]*Ibid.*

[385]*Infra*, 6.4.3.

[386]Dunham/Friedland, p. 389; compare Ireland, pp. 152–153; Prensky, p. 3.

performing mobile tasks. Meanwhile, in an audio-based Flipped Classroom model since students can interact with teachers in the face-to-face sessions, the audio lecture's weakness to develop bonding becomes less relevant. In addition, the audio approach is easier and potentially cheaper as compared with the video approach. The requirement on equipment and technology is the lowest among the three approaches.[387]

Ireland used audio as the media for content delivery in the blended teaching of her Intellectual Property course.[388] She designed her course based on the theory developed by Littlejohn and Pegler who reckon 'wrapping' conventional teaching methods around the e-learning component to provide a 'seamless' learning environment for students.[389] Ireland (re-)designed her Intellectual Property course so that it allowed for close interaction with the audio recording delivered by podcasts.[390] The audio format, instead of video, was used to allow students to read while listening to the recordings.[391] Students were specifically instructed to read the prescribed reading materials and make their own notes, then listen to the audio recordings and compare their notes with the audio content, before attempting the seminar questions.[392] However, Ireland became aware that students 'were listening to the podcasts separately, using iPods or similar portable media players'.[393] Students indicated that it was their preference to be able to use the podcasts independently for amongst other things revision purposes.[394] According to Ireland podcasts have 'improved flexibility' to a whole new level to allow students to engage in 'anytime, anywhere' learning.[395] Blending with podcasts has allowed Ireland to replace almost half of the face-to-face class time.[396]

Dunham and Friedland support the use of podcasts also because this allows the inclusion of supplementary materials designed specifically for the format of the class.[397] They believe that supplementary materials can positively influence student learning outcomes and student performance.[398] Podcasted supplemental material

---

[387]Compare Martin, p. 76.

[388]Ireland, pp. 140–141.

[389]*Ibid*, p. 149.

[390]*Ibid.*

[391]*Ibid.*

[392]*Ibid.*

[393]*Ibid*, p. 150.

[394]*Ibid.*

[395]*Ibid*, p. 152.

[396]*Ibid*, p. 141. For the differences between podcasting and Flipped Classrooms compare *supra*, 2.2.3.

[397]Dunham/Friedland, p. 390.

[398]*Ibid*, pp. 390–391.

can also be used to develop listening skills which is essential in the legal profession.[399] It is important that—like the Ireland study—also Dunham and Friedland's study relates to podcasting[400] and not to the Flipped Classroom concept.

Similarly, the preference for audio over video podcasting was also confirmed in a research project on lecture capture performed by Brittain et al. Students' response was recorded in a survey to test students' preference for particular media formats. The recording of microbiology lectures was posted in three media formats: (1) white board approach, (2) screen capture approach, and (3) audio-only format.[401] The survey results reveal that students preferred audio recordings rather than video due to the perceived increased mobility.[402] It is noteworthy, however, the study of Brittain et al. explores lecture captures and students have presumably attended the face-to-face lectures before reviewing the lectures via audio podcasts. The recording therefore only served as a repeat and the level of concentration required may have been lower.

Finally, audio teaching materials are beneficial to beginners in developing e-learning tools as the technological threshold and the cost of production are comparatively lower.[403] To record, teachers can simply attach a microphone to the computer and software tools are readily available on the Internet.[404] The production costs of audio materials are much lower than materials in video format.[405] If there is indeed little difference in the learning outcomes, audio formats may consequently be preferable.[406]

3.5.4 Conclusions

From a pedagogical point of view there is not yet a definite answer to the question whether video or audio is a better media for the delivery of online lectures. It is all about providing choices to students with different learning styles, i.e. visual and auditory learners as well as availability of resources.

---

[399] *Ibid.*

[400] Compare, *supra* 2.2.3.

[401] Brittain/Glowaki/Van Ittersum/Johnson, p. 26.

[402] *Ibid*, p. 28.

[403] Martin, p. 76.

[404] *Ibid.*

[405] *Ibid*, Brittain/Glowaki/Van Ittersum/Johnson, p. 28.

[406] Martin, p. 77; also see Dey/Burn/Gerdes, p. 390.

3.6 Observations, Potential Problems and Open Questions

3.6.1 General

The previous sections have critically assessed the existing literature on the pedagogical viability of Flipped Classrooms and related topics. This section summarizes the findings and raises additional points.

3.6.2 Limited Data

The Flipped Classroom model is a relatively new approach to teaching and learning and this is particularly true in the area of legal education. As already indicated, literature and research on the usefulness of Flipped Classrooms in legal education is very limited. Most of the research on Flipped Classrooms concentrated on the qualitative rather than quantitative experience to evaluate the quality of learning, with a focus on teachers' or students' perceptions of their own experiences. There is hardly any study on the potential of Flipped Classrooms to improve learning outcomes or the impact of Flipped Classrooms on students' motivation. The available research on learning performances is either small-scale or not in the area of legal education.

The rather comprehensive study of Means et al. on behalf of the U.S. Department of Education on the effectiveness of blended learning can only provide limited information as its main focus is on non-legal education.[407] Though the meta-analysis of Means et al. shows that blended learning leads to better outcomes than learning under face-to-face- and purely online teaching modes, it does not explain reasons why this is the case.[408] For example, the better learning outcomes may have been the result of additional learning time and materials and be unrelated to the teaching mode.[409] In addition, Means et al. are also aware of the inconsistency between their meta-analysis and the narrative review findings. Their narrative review reveals that there are many options to combine online and face-to-face teaching components as well as other options. It may thus be too soon to confirm the success of the blended learning model.[410]

At this point it must be concluded that there is not yet any hard data on the pedagogical feasibility and viability of Flipped Classrooms and the superiority of particular Flipped Classroom formats, e.g the audio or the video format.

---

[407]Compare Means/Toyama/Murphy/Bakia/Jones; also *supra*, 2.2.2.

[408]Hess, p. 70.

[409]Compare Means/Toyama/Murphy/Bakia/Jones, p. 29, Exhibit 5.

[410]*Ibid*, pp. 48–49.

3.6.3 The Flip Sides of Flipped Classrooms

The above literature review has revealed the perceived major advantages of the Flipped Classroom concept. First, the use of Flipped Classrooms can free up time for in-class interactive teaching and learning activities by moving (non-interactive) lecture modules online.[411] It must be considered, however, that this means that the Flipped Classroom concept enlarges the teaching time by adding online lecture time to the in-class time which is used for interactive teaching modules. The question is, if more time for interactive teaching is really needed given the fact that teaching sessions may already be long enough to achieve the required learning outcomes. As one Hong Kong colleague put it, 'we are already struggling to fill the 3 hour sessions.'[412] From the students' perspective the same concerns may apply as the in-class time is supplemented by online lecture time which will come in addition to self-study time. The question is if this leads to a situation where students are 'overtaught'.

Second, Flipped Classrooms allow students to follow lectures anywhere and anytime, i.e. the use of Flipped Classrooms increases learning flexibility.[413] However, flexibility may come at a price as students may not dedicate the same degree of concentration to online lectures watched in a non-classroom environment.[414]

Studies on which we have reported above have pointed out—though without leading to absolute conclusions—the advantages and disadvantages of the traditional lecture mode as opposed to in-class interactivity and thus the advantages of Flipped Classrooms.[415] The general assumption that in-class interactivity in whatever format is desirable, but does not automatically lead to any superiority of the Flipped Classroom model. In contrast, it must be considered how the Flipped Classroom concept compares with the traditional teaching approach under which students are asked to prepare for in-class sessions (conducted by way of lectures or by way of interactive modes) through reading assignments as identified by the teachers or by readings as independently organized by students. The Flipped Classroom concept as we have defined it on the basis of the existing literature[416] entails passive online learning rather than active engagement with the subject matter. In contrast, reading assignments require (or at least: can require) students to prepare for their classes independently. Reading assignments foster active learning much more than online lectures and are therefore much more in line with the idea of deep learning.

---

[411]Compare *supra*, 3.3.1.

[412]The standard length of postgraduate teaching sessions at CUHK Faculty of Law is three hours.

[413]Compare *supra*, 3.3.2.

[414]Compare *supra*, 3.3.9.

[415]*Supra*, 3.2 and 3.3.

[416]*Supra*, 2.3.

Furthermore, from the viewpoint of training law students for practice, reading assignments in preparation of classes resemble the practical work of lawyers to a much greater extent than the passive consumption of online lectures.

It is one of the perceived advantages of Flipped Classrooms that 'digital native' students may enjoy e-learning approaches including Flipped Classrooms. Flipped Classrooms may therefore have motivational/inspirational effects.[417] It is important to emphasize in this context that this aspect carries value only if motivating and inspiring students is really one of the core missions of tertiary education. This assumption can be challenged with good reasons. University students are adults who are free to study or not to study and who should be free to determine their own learning modes. In particular, while the risks involved in independent learning need to be kept in mind, the less guided a course of study is, the more will students benefit from a successful self-organization of their studies.[418] Consequently, one might argue that the motivational and inspirational aspects of the Flipped Classroom concept can well be ignored.

3.6.4 Resistance

3.6.4.1 Teacher Resistance

Different parties may be reluctant to adopt the Flipped Classroom concept. First of all, teachers may not be in favour of the Flipped Classroom concept for a variety of reasons, but in particular because they lack the necessary pedagogical and technical training.[419] Ocak carried out a survey to study why faculty members are unwilling to teach blended courses. Nearly 25 % of the respondents indicated the complexity of the instruction in blended courses.[420] Another 10 % of the respondents felt incompetent to use the relevant technology.[421] Even when training in e-learning was offered by the teachers' home institution, it seldom led to the actual adoption of e-learning modes.[422]

According to Ocak's survey, 17 % of the teacher-respondents in his case study on the introduction of e-learning considered their institutional support

---

[417] *Supra*,1.2.3–4 and 3.3.3.

[418] Compare Lutz-Christian Wolff, Learning without teaching, available at http://www5.cuhk.edu.hk/elearning/expo2013/index.php/summary-archive/presentation-materials (last visited on 22 January 2016).

[419] Compare Blue Paper, p. 34.

[420] Ocak, p. 694.

[421] *Ibid*, p. 697.

[422] Sutton, p. 43.

inadequate,[423] among which almost 10 % stated that there was a lack of effective communication.[424]

Teachers may also be generally opposed to the introduction of new teaching approaches simply because this requires extra work. Furthermore, since it is uncertain how Flipped Classrooms are received by students in particular during an experiential period when the use of this new teaching mode is not perfected yet, the use of Flipped Classrooms may affect teaching evaluations which could be fatal for teachers' careers.[425] Nevertheless, Verkerke encourages first-time teachers to design their courses using Flipped Classroom from scratch. He explains that the longer a teacher teaches, the stronger is the inertia to stick to what is familiar and the more reluctant one becomes to experimenting with new ideas.[426]

3.6.4.2 Institutional Resistance

In environments where the use of new technologies for law teaching purposes is not yet common the institution as a whole may be reluctant to support the use of Flipped Classrooms. Again, this may affect the standing of teachers who nonetheless try out this new teaching approach. Graham et al. explain the reason for lack of recognition of online teaching modes by university administrations being that e-learning strategies are often not implemented at the institutional level, but adopted by individuals.[427] Smith even suggests that law schools sometimes foster technophobia and their poor infrastructure banishes technology from classrooms.[428] Without the proper support from their faculty, law professors are often discouraged to use technological teaching aids.[429]

To fix these problems, Taylor and Newton propose the university-wide implementation of e-learning strategies.[430] Friel et al. encourage the building of training teams to provide technology training in a pedagogical context.[431] To ensure the transfer of skills, they also suggest greater participation of IT staff in staff training programmes, such as one-on-one faculty training between training sessions.[432] To ensure the effective implementation of technology, they also recommend a hotline for immediate problem solving.[433] The University of Central Florida points out that

---

[423] Ocak, p. 696.
[424] *Ibid*, p. 694.
[425] Compare, however, *infra*, 6.5.2.5.
[426] Wood.
[427] Graham/Woodfield/Harrison, p. 4.
[428] Smith, p. 249.
[429] Compare Smith, pp. 256–257; Ocak, p. 696.
[430] Taylor/Newton, p. 57.
[431] Friel/Britten/Compton/Peak/Schoch/VanTyle, p. 302.
[432] *Ibid*.
[433] *Ibid*, p. 306.

'faculty readiness' lies in the heart of effective adoption of technologies.[434] Faculty members need to embrace certain traits so that they can easily adapt to teaching with technologies. Such traits may include:

- 'motivation to learn,
- willingness to lose some control of class design and teaching style,
- ability to collaborate with experts,
- willingness to change role,
- ability to build a support system,
- patience with technology,
- ability to learn from others'.[435]

From an institutional point of view if the introduction of Flipped Classrooms (or other innovative teaching approaches) is sought after, e.g. as part of an e-learning strategy, incentives for teachers and students need to be considered. This may include teaching relieve for the development of Flipped Classrooms and grants to support the acquisition of needed hard and software or to buy-in replacement teachers.

The first-time use of Flipped Classrooms like the first time use of any other teaching method carries the risk of bad teaching evaluations.[436] Institutions that wish to encourage the use of Flipped Classrooms or other experiential teaching methods may consider disregarding teaching evaluations so as not to discourage teachers from trying out these new approaches.

3.6.4.3 Student Resistance

Finally, students may not welcome the use of Flipped Classrooms for different reasons. It can be expected, but not be taken for granted that students are digital natives and competent users of new technologies.[437] Consequently, orientation and technical training to students prior to online classes must be considered.[438] Furthermore, students must understand the structure of the course as well as the (blended) teaching mode and have suitable devices, software and sufficient connectivity to access the video/audio lectures.[439] It is also advisable to check the availability of facilities such as in a computer library to allow access by students who do not possess the devices personally and to provide ongoing technical support.[440]

---

[434]Kaminskaya, p. 20.

[435]*Ibid*, pp. 20–21.

[436]Note, however, that this was not the experience in the case study the authors have conducted, compare *infra*, 6.5.2.5.

[437]*Supra*, 3.3.9.

[438]Blue Paper, p. 35.

[439]*Ibid*.

[440]Ireland, p. 158.

Advice and guidance should be offered to students on how to use the video or audio sessions, with an emphasis on the importance of accessing the online material before coming to class.[441]

Teachers have to understand that students may not be familiar with the Flipped Classroom model. Students may find that this model requires more weekly preparation work. Steps have to be taken which require students to become responsible and independent learners and take the initiative to prepare for classes. The Flipped Classroom concept requires self-discipline in learning. The in-class exercises bear no values unless students engage in meaningful classroom activities.[442] Initial resistance will be alleviated as—and if—students come to appreciate the advantages of Flipped Classrooms.[443] As always, good communication is therefore the key to success.

Finally, culture plays an important role in the learning approach and self-directedness of students.[444] It has been observed that 'Western students tend to feel a greater need for self-direction in academic tasks', whereas Asian students need more structured directions from their teachers.[445] The background of students, e.g in terms of culture and familiarity with e-devices, may consequently affect their adaptability to any kind of e-learning approach. Anecdotal evidence collected by the authors of this book suggests that Asian students may prefer face-to-face lecturing. Self-financed students may expect face-to-face teaching as online lectures may not be regarded as 'value for money'. Again, it must be emphasized in this context that Flipped Classrooms are not meant to replace in-class time. Flipped classrooms rather move lecture modules online to out-of-class time to free in-class time for interactivity.[446] But, if not communicated well, this can be easily misunderstood.

3.6.4.4 Communication Needs

The potential for resistance from the various involved parties calls for strategies to ensure cooperation. Some of the options in this regard were already addressed in previous sections. It appears that the most important aspect is adequate communication. Whether it is an institution that wants to entice teachers to adopt innovative teaching approaches or whether it is a teacher who wishes to convince her employer or students of the benefits of Flipped Classrooms—or at least the benefits of trying out the Flipped Classroom concept—if not explained properly, the new approach is bound to fail.

[441]Compare Upchurch, p. 6; Blue Paper, p. 35.

[442]*Supra*, 3.3.1.

[443]Davis/Neary/Vaughn, p. 18.

[444]Alias, p. 4.

[445]Tweed/Lehman, p. 96 and *passim*.

[446]*Supra*, 2.3.

3.6.5 *Students' Time Constraints*

Special requirements in terms of balancing time between studying and work commitments and sometimes also family responsibilities are required in particular in the postgraduate part-time sector. Many working students may have to put up with long working hours. This leads to the question if the Flipped Classroom concept is feasible for this group of students, i.e. if it is realistic to request them to view video lectures—potentially in addition to the reading assignments—prior to class.

The issue of students' work overload is addressed in the 'Legal Education and Training in Hong Kong: Preliminary Review'.[447] The Report concludes that it is unrealistic and maybe even counter-productive to give students heavy reading assignments.[448] Flipped Classrooms will have to meet similar concerns as it increases the required out-of-class time. And, it goes without saying that the issue of teaching overload applies in the same way to full-time students.

3.6.6 *Law as an Unsuitable Subject for Multiple-Use Online Modules?*

Flipped Classrooms are particularly most suitable from the viewpoint of resource allocation if they are developed for multiple uses. However, in many areas the law is fast changing. In fact, in some areas (such as PRC law) new laws and regulations are enacted almost on a daily basis. In law areas of this kind it would therefore be difficult if not impossible to develop Flipped Classrooms for multiple use and the production of Flipped Classrooms may not be viable.

We have conducted a cursory research on the subjects which have been chosen for 'blended teaching purposes'. We found that with a number of exceptions,[449] online modules are often used to teach Legal Research[450] and Civil or Criminal Procedure.[451] It is unclear why the focus is on these subjects, but it could be that at least the legal research course it is less likely to encounter frequent changes.

---

[447]Redmond/Roper, p. 22.

[448]*Ibid*, p. 25.

[449]Beck uses online lecture for International Law; Ireland for Intellectual Property; Field/Jones for Public Law and Criminal Law; Jones for Legal Environment; Polding for Legal Practice course; Verkerke for Contract.

[450]Davis/Neary/Vaughan; Gerdy et al.; Lemmer; Lihosit/Larrington.

[451]McKeller/Maharg; Slomanson; Upchurch.

3.6.7 Flipped Classrooms and Teacher Personality

Without being able to offer any hard evidence, we feel that the success of university teaching depends very much on the personality of teachers. In other words, teachers' personalities and thus their teaching approach is the most important inspirational and motivational factor in law teaching. This factor is lost in any (static) online teaching tool. Having said that, the Flipped Classroom approach as understood for the purposes of this book[452] does not replace the in-class performance of teachers with online lectures. In contrast, online lectures are to supplement interactive in-class activities.

3.6.8 Flipped Classrooms to Deepen Particular Subject Areas

The Flipped Classroom approach may allow deepening areas and topics which cannot be sufficiently covered in-class due to time constraints. For example, in relation to the Juris Doctor programme offered in Hong Kong (which is a fast-track law study programme for students who already hold an undergraduate degree) the legal profession has sporadically voiced concerns that some subjects are not taught with the sufficient depth. These concerns could be addressed by adding online teaching modules. Their goal would be, however, to add (online) teaching time rather than freeing in-class time for interactivity and they would consequently not qualify as Flipped Classrooms as defined above.

3.6.9 Searching for the One and Only Teaching Mode: Mission Impossible?

The discussion in the previous sections revealed that different teaching methods do have advantages and disadvantages. Furthermore, the suitability of different teaching methods depends very much on the particular teaching environment and last but not least the teacher herself and the respective students. Even within particular classes the student body may often be very diverse. Particular teaching modes may work for one group of students, but not for others. In classes with a diverse student body it may therefore in fact be impossible to adopt the one and only teaching method that suits all students. And, all this applies of course also to Flipped Classrooms and thus limits the potential of success of this concept.

[452] *Supra*, 2.3.

Law teacher may have to accept that a perfect pedagogy does not exist. In contrast, what it takes to make a course successful lies in individual teachers' ability to adopt different teaching methods catered to the particular setting of a class and teachers' willingness to improve teaching methods on the basis of their own flexibility.[453]

[453]Compare Laster, p. 273; Le Brun/Johnstone, pp. 313–314.

Chapter 4
How to Develop Flipped Classrooms?

4.1 General

The previous chapter has focused on the pedagogical viability of Flipped Classrooms. This chapter now discusses how Flipped Classrooms can be developed and thus the technical viability of the Flipped Classroom concept.

The development of Flipped Classrooms involves three steps: (1) Planning, (2) Production and (3) Distribution.[1] These steps are explored in more detail one by one in the following. A checklist in Appendix B summarizes the main points and is meant to facilitate the development of Flipped Classrooms.

In the context of our Flipped Classroom project we have actually flipped some lectures as a pilot study to assess the level of difficulty incurred during the production process and related issues.[2] Our experience[3] has led us to conclude that it is in fact rather easy to produce video lectures thus confirming basic assumptions on which we report in this chapter.

4.2 Planning

A successful Flipped Classroom requires detailed planning.[4] Understanding the purpose of 'flipping' the classroom is the first important step. On the basis of a clear vision of the educational goals to be achieved by flipping,[5] teachers should consider

[1]Deakin Learning Futures Teaching Development Team, p. 10.
[2]Compare *infra*, Chap. 6.
[3]*Infra*, 6.4.7.
[4]*Ibid*, p. 10.
[5]*Ibid.*

L.-C. Wolff and J. Chan, *Flipped Classrooms for Legal Education*,
SpringerBriefs in Law, DOI 10.1007/978-981-10-0479-7_4

the desired student learning outcomes. In contrast, technology should not drive the course design.[6]

Teachers are advised to 'start small'.[7] It is unnecessary to flip the entire course right from the beginning.

> You don't have to commit to this model for an entire semester. Pick one unit of material and apply the flipped classroom model to this unit. For example, you might decide to choose a unit that the students find challenging. The additional benefit from the videos on this material will have a positive effect on your class. You can start even smaller with flipping what you would normally lecture to clear up confusion in a single class.[8]

The choice of the content suitable to be delivered by video/audio lectures is important. Content that contains 'straight forward concept, basic application, or demonstration of a skill' is usually best-suited for flipping.[9] 'Content that is confusing, yet can be previewed to assist class discussion' may also suitable.[10] According to Upchurch, 'some examples of material well-suited for flipping include: preview and review of concepts; summary of law or prior cases; basic concepts or theory; legal definitions; basic skills to be modeled or discussed; basic problems and application of law; and feedback on assignments'.[11] She warns against flipping content that is adequately covered by printed materials, where student enquiries cannot be predicted, where it is difficult to cover the material by a ten minute online modules or where contents do not allow the presentation in the online format.[12]

Video/audio lectures should not be considered as separate structural components from in-class activities but as an integrated part of the design. Dewey advises teachers to determine carefully which components are best delivered by the pre-class lecture and which are best reserved for in-class activities.[13] Upchurch adds that teachers should attempt to optimize and thus enrich the in-class time, rather than teaching students additional content.[14] From her teaching experience, students appreciate in-class activities that provide guided and advanced training on the same topics contained in the videos.[15] In-class activities may include teacher-directed questions and answers, student-directed small group discussion and problem-solving, simulations, whereas pre-lecture content may include not only video/audio but also assigned reading materials.[16] Upchurch also advises to 'provide students

[6]Hess, p. 79.

[7]Upchurch, p. 5.

[8]*Ibid*; compare CADQ, pp. 2–3; Dewey, p. 2.

[9]Upchurch, p. 4.

[10]*Ibid*.

[11]*Ibid*, pp. 4–5.

[12]*Ibid*, p. 4.

[13]Dewey, p. 3.

[14]Upchurch, p. 5.

[15]*Ibid*.

[16]*Ibid*; Dewey, p. 4.

with tasks to complete while watching or immediately after watching the video' to reinforce the learning.[17] Harmonizing a variety of learning activities, such as individual work, group discussion and presentation, simulation and brief lectures requires experience. Davis et al. describe the experience of 'flipping' the classroom as imposing a learning curve on teachers. However, over time and with increased practice teachers will become more skilled in avoiding and addressing difficulties.[18]

Teachers have to decide on the length of each recording. How much time will students have to commit prior to class? Le Brun and Johnstone remark that 'students lose concentration after about 20 minutes'.[19] In fact, a number of law teachers have reportedly produced recordings lasting only between 10 to 20 min.[20] However, a recent empirical study on the relationship between viewing and student's attitudes suggests that students may prefer longer videos.[21] According to this study the student preferred duration of video lectures vary from 15 to 100 min with an average at 37.41 min.[22] In any event, teachers have to consider whether any additional amount of out-of-class work is realistic. Teachers should be mindful that an unrealistic workload will result in a decrease in motivation.[23] And, the ultimate purpose of flipping is to enhance learning, not to increase the workload.[24] Finally, there is also a practical reason for keeping the recording short as this reduces the time necessary for downloading the file. Smaller files are easier to access, i.e. within a reasonable time.[25]

Planning also involves the decision whether to use the 'white board approach', the 'screen capture approach' or an audio-only format. Specifics of these different formats have been discussed above.[26] Once the decision is made it is advisable to consult with IT experts for technical assistance. Questions such as, whether the necessary equipment or technology is available, whether or not additional investment is necessary, the availability of a studio or assigned site for recording are important factors as they may affect the implementation and even the decision on which mode to use.[27] As 'some of the screencast programs require substantial memory and may crash when run on a laptop', it may be best to develop Flipped Classrooms on a desktop computer.[28] Some editing software is more compatible with particular operating systems. Examples are Windows Movie Maker for PCs or

[17]Upchurch, p. 6.
[18]Davis/Neary/Vaughn, p. 18.
[19]Le Brun/Johnstone, p. 260.
[20]Davis/Neary/Vaughn, p. 14; Ireland, p. 150; McKellar/Maharg, p. 48; Upchurch, p. 5.
[21]Giannakos/Jaccheri/Krogstie, p. 12.
[22]*Ibid*, p. 8.
[23]Redmond/Roper, p. 35.
[24]Dewey, p. 3.
[25]Ireland, p. 150.
[26]*Supra*, 3.5.2 and 3.5.3.
[27]Dewey, p. 3.
[28]Lihosit/Larrington, p. 10, footnote 13.

iMovie for Mac PCs.[29] The choice of the desktop computer therefore becomes an important factor.[30] Some editing software may be on offer 'at a discounted institutional rate or even at no cost as part of an institutional subscription'.[31] It is necessary to check which subscriptions the university has.[32]

Lastly, some academics warn that the planning of Flipped Classrooms and the work on technical aspects can be labour-intensive and time-consuming.[33] Law teachers are therefore advised to ensure that sufficient time is available prior to starting the production of Flipped Classrooms.[34] It should be pointed out, however, that our own experience did not confirm these concerns at all as explained further below.[35]

4.3 Production

4.3.1 General

It is normally prudent for teachers to prepare a script before recording.[36] During the recording teachers should speak with precision and clarity.[37] Before recording, teachers are advised to practice 'speaking aloud to get a feel for the script' and its length.[38] Recordings should be divided into mini-lectures capping at ten-minutes for easy access and review.[39] If a recording studio is not an option, teachers are advised to consider carefully the location of the video recording.[40] Teachers can also choose to record at their desk but they are advised to experiment with the lighting to ensure best picture quality.[41] Background sounds in the room may be distracting and affect the quality of the recording. It goes without saying that during the recording in an office the voicemail of a desk phone should be turned on and mobile phones as well as sound-generating devices should be turned off.[42]

---

[29]Deakin Learning Futures Teaching Development Team, p. 20.

[30]Compare Lihosit/Larrington, p. 10.

[31]*Ibid.*

[32]*Ibid.*

[33]Beck, p. 279.

[34]Dewey, p. 2; Ireland, p. 155; Beck, 279; Davis/Neary/Vaughn, p. 18.

[35]*Infra*, 6.4.7.

[36]Deakin Learning Futures Teaching Development Team, p. 11, Module 2, Table 1.

[37]Blue Paper, p. 26.

[38]Deakin Learning Futures Teaching Development Team, p. 14.

[39]Blue Paper, p. 27; Upchurch, p. 5.

[40]Deakin Learning Futures Teaching Development Team, p. 17.

[41]*Ibid.*

[42]*Ibid.*

Teachers should not aim at perfect video or audio recordings. Upchurch advises that recordings should be made in one take and teachers should avoid obsession with editing out the 'ums' and small errors.[43] For video recordings, unnecessary motion or irrelevant images that may distract students should be avoided.[44] It may be helpful to experiment with the recording first to ensure satisfaction with the quality.[45]

As mentioned earlier,[46] there are three common formats of online lectures, i.e. the 'white board approach', 'screen capture approach' or the 'audio-only format'. We had introduced related pedagogical considerations above.[47] The following sections will now focus on technical aspects and practical issues. The selection of a particular format will ultimately depend on teachers' own technical strengths, the available time and resources as well as students' preference.[48]

4.3.2 White Board Approach

The 'white board approach' can be implemented by video-recording a teacher's lecture in front of a webcam or a video camera.

A webcam is an easy way to make a video.[49] A short video of a teacher's presentation can even be produced with the webcam of laptop or desktop computer. Webcam produced videos are ideal to present short content, such as 'welcome messages, to introduce topics, provide overviews and address frequently asked questions'.[50] Should it be necessary to edit the video a special video editing software, such as iMovie or Windows Movie Maker, would be required.[51] For the purpose of ensuring a sufficient audio recording quality the recording device of a computer must be checked upfront.[52] Internal and external microphones may provide different quality levels with external devices usually being the better choice.[53]

As an easy alternative, recording can also be done by using a proper video camera or the inbuilt camera on a mobile device.[54] There are plenty of products in

---

[43]Upchurch, p. 5.

[44]*Ibid*, pp. 5–6.

[45]Compare *infra*, 6.4.7.

[46]Compare, *supra* 3.5.

[47]*Ibid.*

[48]Compare for the considerations regarding the decision of our case study *infra*, 6.4.3.

[49]Deakin Learning Futures Teaching Development Team, p. 17.

[50]*Ibid.*

[51]*Ibid.*

[52]*Ibid.*

[53]*Ibid.*

[54]*Ibid*, p. 18.

the market with varying recording quality.[55] Subject to availability, it is of course advisable to choose one which provides higher quality recording for a more sophisticated production.[56]

Editing apps usually come with the video camera or mobile device. But these apps may have different and sometimes limited editing features.[57] iMovie and Pinnacle Studio are apps for the iOS platform and Magisto and Vid Trim Pro are apps for the Android platform.[58] The editing of the video on a computer requires an editing software such as Windows Movie Maker for PCs operating on Windows or iMovie for Mac.[59]

4.3.3 Screen Capture Approach

Screen capture recordings allow teacher's voice to be recorded separately from the presentation. Screen capture recordings provide explanations and examples around a bullet point slideshows.[60] The making of videos by 'screen capture approach' requires screencasting software, such as Camstasia, Captivate, Echo 360 Personal Capture, Educreations, Jing, MediaSite, Screener, Screencast-O-Matic and Snagit.[61] The user-friendliness of different screencasting software may differ and should be assessed carefully.[62] Lihosit and Larrington explain that some of these tools are 'extremely intuitive and easy to learn … others have robust editing capabilities.'[63] They chose Echo 360 for their Flipped Classroom project because the software was available free and, has a very simple interface as well as simple editing capability.[64]

4.3.4 Audio-Only Format

Audio recording is a quick and effective way to deliver a lecture online. It requires a mobile device, such as a smartphone or tablet to record a message.[65] The quality of

[55]*Ibid.*

[56]*Ibid.*

[57]*Ibid*, p. 20.

[58]*Ibid*, p. 20, Module 2, Table 6.

[59]*Ibid*, p. 20.

[60]*Ibid*, p. 21; *supra*, 3.5.1.

[61]Compare *ibid*, p. 21, Module 2, Table 7; Lihosit/Larrington, p. 10; Davis/Neary/Vaughn, p. 14.

[62]Davis/Neary/Vaughn, p. 18·

[63]Lihosit/Larrington, p. 10.

[64]*Ibid*, p. 11; compare *infra*, 6.4.4 for the authors' choice.

[65]Deakin Learning Futures Teaching Development Team, p. 15.

sound should approximate to FM radio for optimal listening.[66] Mobile devices usually come with simple editing apps. However, more sophisticated editing may not be available.[67] Some common voice recording apps for iOS are Recordium and Voice Recorder HD.[68] For Android Voice Pro and Voice Recorder Pro are available.[69] Editing on a computer is possible via audio editing applications, such as Audacity for a PC or GarageBand for a Mac.[70]

4.3.5 Students' Preference

Students' preferences are important when selecting the delivery mode of online lectures. Teachers need to know what devices students will use for viewing of or listening to online lectures. This is to ensure that the video/audio formats chosen are compatible with students' devices, operating systems and browsers.[71]

Common media players potentially available for students to be used to view online lectures are QuickTime, Flash, WMP, and RealPlayer.[72] According to Beck's study though video podcasts were popular among students, Flash was selected by the majority.[73] Giannakos et al's empirical studies on the relationship between viewing and student's attitudes show that YouTube is preferred over university's video platforms.[74] In fact, most students value the use of social media such as Facebook, Twitter and Google+ to assist learning.[75] Giannakos et al's findings also indicate that the majority of students (75 %) watch video lectures prior to the exam period.[76] Obviously, the more students believe that video lectures will improve their examination results the more they will watch the online lectures.[77] To accommodate students with various learning needs, the Blue Paper advises to provide a written transcript for any video posted.[78]

---

[66] Audacity, under Sample Rates.

[67] Deakin Learning Futures Teaching Development Team, p. 15.

[68] *Ibid*, p. 15, Module 2, Table 5.

[69] *Ibid.*

[70] *Ibid*, p. 16.

[71] Compare Blue Paper, p. 20.

[72] Lihosit/Larrington, p. 10.

[73] Beck, p. 278.

[74] Giannakos/Jaccheri/Krogstie, p. 10.

[75] *Ibid,* p. 9.

[76] *Ibid*, p.12.

[77] *Ibid.*

[78] Blue Paper, pp. 20, 27.

4.4 Distribution

Once the video or audio recordings are finalized it is necessary to enable students to access the file(s). A high bandwidth is required for uploading and downloading if files are of large size as it is often the case for good quality videos. Some law schools have existing online platforms (Blackboard, WebCT, and TWEN) which allow uploading of digital files without the need of additional investment.[79] It is mandatory to consult with IT staff to clarify certain issues regarding the use of these platforms for distribution purposes:

Is ‘streaming’ available? Streaming allows students to view or listen to files while at the same time downloading the file without having to wait for the download to be complete.[80] The availability of streaming technology would shorten the time for accessing the files and most certainly improve user experience.[81]

The resolution and the quality of sound are directly important for the file size. Teachers need to take into account that higher quality comes with issues of size and distribution.[82] Since it is normally unknown at what time students will access online lectures, there is at least the theoretical possibility that many students taking the course may access the file at the same time. As a precautionary measure, the bandwidth of the portals should therefore be wide enough to accommodate simultaneous access.[83] If this is not possible, the limit on access numbers must be known in advance to allocate access time slots to students.

Furthermore, it is important to ascertain that the server has enough storage for all the digital files and whether a particular storage quota can be allocated to the ‘flipped’ course.

It is also advisable to study institutional policies regarding the uploading and downloading of digital files, if any are in place. Vice versa, from an institutional perspective it may be prudent to consider the development of related policies to create a framework for the development of e-learning strategies at different levels. Such a policy may address issues such as data privacy, intellectual property rights,[84] quality assurance,[85] financial arrangements,[86] special arrangements regarding teaching and course evaluations as well as incentives for teachers to adopt e-learning tools.

---

[79]*Ibid*, p. 19.

[80]Compare Woodford.

[81]Blue Paper, p. 14.

[82]Audacity, under Quality Preferences; video file size calculators are available online, compare e.g. Peter Forret.

[83]Blue Paper, p. 20.

[84]*Ibid*, p. 390.

[85]*Ibid*, p. 36.

[86]*Ibid*, p. 41.

In case the institutional IT department prefers hosting the files by other means, the option of private platforms is available.[87] It is common for teachers to host videos using private platforms such as YouTube or podcasting to facilitate student access. But, since this type of open channel makes the files publicly accessible, teachers may consider engaging the help of IT staff for the protection of digital files.[88] Other sharing platforms are Vimeo and SoundCloud. Vimeo is known for its large creative community and SoundCloud is an online audio sharing platform.[89] Online storage services are also available, such as Portfolio, OneDrive for Business, GoogleDrive and Cloudstor.[90]

4.5 Technical Challenges

According to various case studies including our own,[91] the recording and editing of video/audio lectures is not technically challenging. However, the process is often described by academics as labour-intensive and time-consuming.[92] The main reason is the lack of teachers' experience in regard to the use of editing software.[93] Also, as already mentioned above,[94] the recording normally takes longer than expected and this is true even for experienced teachers.[95] Tomei conducted a study on the increase in the teaching load when using the online instruction mode. According to his findings online teaching demands a minimum of 14 % more time than traditional teaching modes.[96] According to Ireland, an Intellectual Property course 'of 21 hours lecture-style content delivered via podcasts and 18 hours of face-to-face seminars', took her 350 hours to redesign, including recording and editing, building the website and producing the new seminar guide and problems.[97] Slomanson advises teachers to allow sufficient time for familiarizing with the e-learning tools and software before flipping in order to reduce the likelihood to experience major challenges.[98]

---

[87]Lihosit/Larrington, p. 10.

[88]Blue Paper, p. 27.

[89]Deakin Learning Futures Teaching Development Team, p. 13, Module 2, Table 3.

[90]*Ibid*, p. 13, Module 2, Table 4.

[91]Compare *infra*, 6.5.2 4 (7).

[92]Beck, p. 279.

[93]Compare Davis/Neary/Vaughn, p. 18; Ireland, p. 158.

[94]*Supra*, 4.2.

[95]Compare Ireland, p. 158; Dewey, p. 2.

[96]Tomei, p. 540.

[97]Ireland, pp. 147, 155.

[98]Slomanson, p. 102.

Chapter 5
Costs

5.1 General

The viability of the Flipped Classrooms depends of course also on costs. In this chapter, we attempt to estimate the cost required for the development of Flipped Classrooms and to assess whether Flipped Classrooms are cost-effective from the institutional viewpoint as well as for teaching staff and students.

A literature search on cost evaluation regarding Flipped Classrooms showed that current case studies mostly address distance education. In contrast, few studies are available which have conducted a cost-analysis of the Flipped Classroom concept or—at least—an analysis of the costs for the production of online lectures. In the following we therefore also draw upon studies on cost issues conducted in relation to secondary education. We also explore from a more general point of view whether technology can save cost in education in the long run. Finally, we discuss in this chapter the cost implications of the use of open educational resources as an alternative to the production of Flipped Classrooms in the video or audio format from scratch.

5.2 Costs to Develop Flipped Classrooms

According to Lemmer, unlike other e-learning tools, the technology for creating video lectures is widely available and relatively inexpensive.[1] In contrast, Snowden has drawn attention to concerns about the costs involved in the Flipped Classroom model because of the requirement of resources such as a website, video lectures, worksheets and the time spent on course development.[2] As the level of infrastructure varies between different institutions, the actual costs required for delivery of online

[1]Lemmer, p. 490.
[2]Snowden, p. 12.

L.-C. Wolff and J. Chan, *Flipped Classrooms for Legal Education*,
SpringerBriefs in Law, DOI 10.1007/978-981-10-0479-7_5

components can vary significantly and it is difficult to estimate the precise budget required for the development and delivery of Flipped Classrooms in general terms.[3]

Cohen and Nachmias (2006) explain that the complications in studying cost effectiveness models arise from the fact that academics take different cost effectiveness approaches to online learning.[4] They also point out that there is a lack of systematic data collection. Sometimes fundamental costs are hidden or confidential and cost changes rapidly following the advance in technology makes the task even more difficult.[5] According to them the most common cost components for Web-supported academic instruction are

- costs of human resources,
- support and training,
- general administration costs,
- development, creation and delivery costs,
- central equipment, place and storage costs, and
- usage costs.[6]

Battaglino et al., have compared the cost in virtual—and blended—schools with the traditional 'brick-and-mortar schooling' to study whether online learning can be better and less expensive. Their study targets public-school (elementary, middle and high school) expenditures in the U.S. and found that that the average cost per student for blended learning (US $8,900) is (US $1,100) cheaper than the traditional model (US $10,000) but (US $2,500) more expensive than the fully virtual model (US $6,400).[7] Labour costs take up most of the expenditure in all traditional, blended and virtual models. It also contributes to the biggest saving for blended learning or virtual learning as opposed to the traditional model.[8] Labour costs are made up by the number of teachers and related costs. Blended- and virtual-models often incur two additional, special cost factors, i.e. training costs and IT support costs.[9] Before teachers introduce blended models, training is often required and blended—and virtual—models require additional IT support in particular during the implementation phase.[10] Since blended models are part-onsite, part-offsite, schools are unlikely to experience cost savings in terms of reduced administrative expenses[11] and costs for the use of premises. In fact, even if some of the costs for administrative staff can be lowered, this reduction is partially offset by the increase

---

[3]Lambert/Brewer, p. 73.

[4]Cohen/Nachmias 2006, p. 82.

[5]*Ibid.*

[6]*Ibid*, p. 83.

[7]Battaglino/Haldeman/Laurans, p. 4, Figure. 1.

[8]Compare *ibid*, p. 5.

[9]*Ibid.*

[10]*Ibid.*

[11]*Ibid*, p. 7.

in IT labour cost.[12] Blended-and virtual- models do not necessarily require significant expenditures on technology, depending on what infrastructure already exists.[13]

5.3 Can Technologies Save Cost?

Cohen and Nachmias (2009) implemented a quantitative cost effectiveness analyzer for online academic instruction that was developed at Tel Aviv University.[14] Costs and benefits of 3,453 courses were analyzed in the year 2007.[15] During this year, 23,352 students were enrolled with 1,850 instructors available to them.[16] The findings of this study show that total costs of US $1,350,000 were incurred by online teaching resulting in savings of US $11,255,320.[17] 95 % of these savings had to be attributed to time saved by students 'as a result of electronic content consumption efficiency, receiving/delivering electronic announcements, performing exercises on-line, posting papers and assignments on the Web, and saving copying/printing costs'.[18] In summary, the study shows that the integration of Web-supported instruction is not very cost intensive. The biggest cost factors are teachers who have to spend time and efforts in learning and redesigning the instructions. Being able to use a learning management system at very low costs, students benefit the most. The university invested 'at a relatively low cost in technological and operational infrastructure, gained prestige and improved its instructors' knowledge management'.[19]

When class-size increase and teaching quality assessment and quality assurance mechanisms become standard features of tertiary education, institutions increasingly rely on technology for cost reduction.[20] There is a recent trend in re-usable learning resources as a way to increase institutional efficiency.[21] The re-usable nature of digital educational resources is something that traditional teaching components do not offer. As a commitment to expand blended learning, the University of Wollongang has consequently been exploring ways to re-use digital learning

---

[12]*Ibid.*

[13]*Ibid*, p. 9.

[14]Cohen/Nachmias 2009, p. 1.

[15]*Ibid.*, p. 3.

[16]*Ibid*, pp. 2–3.

[17]*Ibid.*, Table 1, p. 4. Savings are calculated as the sum of efficiency achieved by students, instructors and the university.

[18]*Ibid*, p. 4.

[19]*Ibid.*

[20]Compare Catley, under 'Background'.

[21]Lambert/Brewer, p. 70.

resources.[22] The pilot scheme started with non-law disciplines modeling a work-place simulation after what had been used in a Practical Legal Training (PLT) program.[23]

A number of academics anticipate the re-use of video lectures. In their process of designing a Virtual Learning Environment (VLE), Mckellar and Maharg also recognize that the use of video lectures can save cost when incorporated in an appropriate VLE. Since the material can be re-used, it also increases the accessibility of information and improves the level of knowledge construed by learners.[24] Ireland supports the view that a 'word-perfect iteration' video is a good investment since 'a very high quality iteration is something one can feel comfortable re-using in future offerings'.[25] On the other hand, Davis et al. warn about the practicality as some videos may have a short shelf life and question whether it is worth the effort of spending long hours on recording and editing.[26] To address this risk, Slomanson avoided references to cases in his videos.[27] We had already addressed the potential for problems regarding the re-usability of online modules in law teaching and refer in this regard to our explanations above.[28]

5.4 Open Educational Resources (OERs)

To avoid the investment required in developing video/audio lectures, some educators may choose to use resources readily available on the Internet. For example, as early as in 2003/04, the Oxford Institute of Legal Practice started to use webcasting and podcasting to replace traditional lectures when teaching Financial Services and Markets Act 2000 for the Legal Practice Course.[29]

Online resources can be held in scholarly databases, libraries, or be found on the open web as OERs. OERs are digitalized educational materials that are either (1) released under an open copyright license (e.g. Creative Commons) or (2) are available in the public domain.[30] OERs are offered freely for educators, students, self-learners and any other person to use, 'revise, remix, reuse and redistribute' for teaching, learning and research purpose.[31] Common forms of OERs are:

---

[22] *Ibid*, pp. 72–73.

[23] *Ibid*, p. 71.

[24] McKellar/Mcharg, pp. 43–44.

[25] Ireland, p. 158.

[26] Davis/Neary/Vaughn, p. 18.

[27] Slomanson, p. 97.

[28] *Supra*, 3.6.6.

[29] Polding, pp. 5–6.

[30] Wiley/Green, p. 81.

[31] *Ibid*; Wenk, p. 435.

- '*Learning content* (e.g. courses, modules, learning objects, exercises, references to collections and archives).
- *Software* (e.g. development tools, tools for organizing content and simulation tools).

  ...
- *An implementation resource* (e.g. creative common licenses, best practice design principles).
- *Interperability standard* (e.g. the sharable content object reference model SCORM, the IMS content packaging specification).
- media (e.g. images, audio recordings, videos).'[32]

Examples of OERs include:

- iTunes U where students can find free online courses from institutions around the world, e.g. Harvard on iTunes, Stanford on iTunes[33];
- YouTube EDU where students can find more than 200 lectures on topics ranging from education, science, business, social sciences and arts[34];
- MERLOT—Multimedia and Educational Resources for Learning and Online Teaching[35];
- OpenCourseWare, which was launched by the Massachusetts Institute of Technology in 2009 with the aim of publishing materials from all its courses on the open Web.[36]

The origins of OERs trace back to the growing use of information technologies in the 1980s when academics started sharing digital contents.[37] The expansion of the Internet and the emergence of the World Wide Web have propelled the OER movement to what it is today.[38] In fact, formal educational portals are not the only source for OERs. Individuals can also post OERs through a range of sites operated by third parties and related services, such as YouTube, Slideshare and Academia.edu.[39]

UNESCO addressed the important role of OERs for ensuring wide access to quality higher education in developing countries.[40] The main advantage of OERs is

---

[32]Wenk, p. 436 (footnotes in the text omitted by the authors).

[33]Harvard on iTunes U website.U. http://www.harvard.edu/itunes; Stanford on iTunes U website. https://itunes.stanford.edu/ (both last visited on 25 August 2015).

[34]YouTube EDU website. https://www.youtube.com/channel/UC3yA8nDwraeOfnYfBWun83g (last vistied on 25 August 2015).

[35]MERLOT II website. California State University System, MERLOT II. http://www.merlot.org/merlot/index.htm (last visited on 25 August 2015).

[36]MIT Courseware website, Massachusetts University. http://ocw.mit.edu/index.htm (last visited on 25 August 2015).

[37]Lane/McAndrew, p. 953.

[38]*Ibid.*

[39]Adams/Liyanagunawardena/Rassool/Williams, p. 149.

[40]See UNESCO, UNESCO promotes new initiative for free educational resources on the Internet (8 July 2002). http://www.unesco.org/education/news_en/080702_free_edu_ress.shtml (last visited on 25 August 2015).

that by reusing educational materials prepared by others and made available online, teachers can significantly reduce the preparation time and costs.[41] OERs can also improve the learning experience. 'The resulting variety of materials (and didactical concepts) also stimulates students.'[42] Since they are openly accessible, OERs have become popular among modern students. OERs were the number-one technology that students indicated they wished teachers to use more in a 2012 survey.[43] In fact, the idea of adding social networks as educational tools is catching up fast as universities recognize the potential to use the networks for presenting teaching resources to students.[44]

Despite popularity among students, OERs are less well-received by most faculty when deciding what resources to use. Only 15.3 % of the users of MIT Open Courseware content are educators, 31.4 % are students and 48.2 % are self-learners.[45] There are several reasons for this:

First, it may be difficult and special efforts may be required to integrate 'foreign' resources into ones' own lectures. In fact, this can be more time-consuming than to develop materials from scratch.[46] Second, teachers may encounter technical barriers, such as no access to the repository or wrong document formats. Most importantly, it may be very difficult to find suitable resources[47] as the experience of the authors has confirmed.[48] According to a survey conducted at two universities in Florida, only 7 % of respondents were 'very familiar with open access textbooks, while 52 % were not at all familiar'.[49] Third, '[m]any faculty see these "free" texts as somehow second-rate or commercial house rejects, or think they are only long-out-of-print text.'[50] Forth, the use of copyrighted online resources may be limited to a certain extent.[51]

Online resources are usually protected by copyrights if in the public domain, or available under a Creative Common license.[52] Protection under a copyright is more restrictive and prohibits copying or reusing the work without permission of the copyright owner.[53] In contrast, the Creative Commons regime may allow sharing and sometimes re-arranging of work depending on the terms of the license.[54] Many

---

[41]Wenk, p. 437.

[42]*Ibid.*

[43]Dahlstrom, p. 12.

[44]Micolich, p. 1.

[45]Potts, p. 21, slide.

[46]Wenk, p. 437; also compare for the author's own experience *infra* 6.4.5.3.

[47]*Ibid*, p. 438.

[48]*Infra*, 6.4.5.3.

[49]Morris-Babb/Henderson, p. 151.

[50]*Ibid*, p. 150.

[51]Wenk, p. 438.

[52]Micolich, pp. 2–7.

[53]*Ibid*, pp. 2–3.

[54]See Creative Commons website, under 'license'. http://creativecommons.org/ (last visited on 25 August 2015).

online resources include terms of use, which state which copyright law or Creative Commons rules apply, and to what extent material can be legally reused.[55] Since copyright laws vary from country to country, teachers are advised to check local legislation or with their institution before using online resources.[56] A safer way for utilizing an online resource for educational purpose may be to provide a hyperlink (URL) only.[57]

Since the use of OERs will not be effective when the chosen resource is too long or—at least partly—lacks relevance one may consider editing the online resource to improve relevance for optimal display. However, this again has to be in line with the applicable copyright law or the terms of a license.[58]

The most recent trend in the development of OERs are MOOCs. MOOC stands for Massive Open Online Courses.[59] 'MOOCs are online, free and offer learning materials that can be modified, reused and redistributed to reach massive communities.'[60] MOOCs can provide video lectures, readings, online quizzes, problem sets and learning community forums for interaction.[61] According to Colbran and Gilding MOOCs appeal to educators because they are marketing tools to attract potential future students[62] and promote reputation of the offering institution.[63]

Central Queensland University in Australia has launched a Bachelor of law degree by distance learning mode.[64] Lecture podcasts are available on iTunesU[65] in an open access[66] mode. Other course materials are made publicly available in other ways.[67]

---

[55]Micolich, p. 7.

[56]*Ibid*, p. 2.

[57]*Ibid*, p. 4.

[58]*Ibid*, p. 5.

[59]MOOC website. http://mooc.org/; also see e.g. www.academicroom.com; www.coursera.org; www.edx.org/; www.khanacademy.org/; www.udacity.com (all last visited on 4 September 2015).

[60]Colbran/Gilding, p. 407.

[61]*Ibid*, p. 409.

[62]*Ibid*, p. 406.

[63]*Ibid*.

[64]Central Queensland University website at https://www.cqu.edu.au/courses-and-programs/study-areas/business,-accounting-and-law/undergraduate/bachelor-of-laws (last visited on 4 September 2015).

[65]iTunesU website. https://itunes.apple.com/au/course/ (last visited on 4 September 2015).

[66]See Colbran/Gilding, p. 414. The key difference between 'open source' and 'open access' is that while open-sourced materials can be edited, extended and used by any participants, open access materials can be accessed but not edited.

[67]Colbran/Gilding, p. 413.

Chapter 6
Case Study: Flipped Classrooms for 'The Law of International Business Transactions II'

6.1 General

Previous chapters have discussed theoretical and practical aspects of Flipped Classrooms. This chapter now reflects on the establishment of Flipped Classrooms as a pilot project in relation to the course on 'The Law of International Business Transactions II' (LIBT II) in Term II of the academic year 2014/15. LIBT II is a compulsory subject for students enrolled in the Master of Laws in International Economic Law programme (IEL) offered by the Faculty of Law of the Chinese University of Hong Kong (CUHK).[1] LIBT II can also be chosen as an elective course by students of the Juris Doctor programme offered by the CUHK Faculty of other Master of Laws programmes and Law.

The purpose of this chapter is twofold. First it demonstrates how classrooms can be 'flipped' and how the Flipped Classroom concept can consequently be used in practice by conducting a case study. In fact, our case study was meant to apply and thus to test the findings of the previous chapters as to the viability in terms of technical, financial and other resource related aspects 'on the ground'. By explaining how we have developed Flipped Classrooms in the LIBT II context a framework is developed which we hope can be translated into more general terms and thus be used for any future law course offering.

Second, our case study was also aimed to test our findings regarding the pedagogical viability of Flipped Classrooms in legal education. For this purpose, we have not only 'flipped' two of the LIBT II lecture modules but also tried to evaluate the success of our 'flipping' experience. Again, when translated into general terms the evaluation framework used for this purpose should be fit for use also in the context of any other law course offering. The chance to improve the LIBT II itself course was a welcome by-product of the case study.

---

[1]For details see *infra*, 6.2.

L.-C. Wolff and J. Chan, *Flipped Classrooms for Legal Education*,
SpringerBriefs in Law, DOI 10.1007/978-981-10-0479-7_6

The structure of this chapter is as follows:

We first offer some necessary background information regarding the LIBT II course and our reasons for flipping the LIBT II classroom. This is followed by the discussion of how Flipped LIBT II Classrooms could be and have in fact been developed. In the second part of this chapter we explain how we have evaluated the use of Flipped Classrooms in the LIBT II context to support and refine the findings of our study.

6.2 The LIBT II Course

6.2.1 Course Contents

The LIBT II course has been offered at postgraduate level in Hong Kong for more than ten years. The LIBT II course concerns the law of cross-border investments whereas a LIBT I course covers legal aspects of non-investment related cross-border business transactions.[2] Both courses focus on transactional aspects, i.e. the question how international business transactions are conducted in practice, and on the legal questions arising out of different areas of law at the different transaction stages.

The LIBT II course takes a holistic approach and aims to provide a structured introduction to the theoretical and practical aspects of the law governing cross-border business transactions.[3] It is one of the major goals of the LIBT II course to demonstrate the interconnectivity of different substantive law topics during particular stages of various transaction types. Topics covered under the LIBT II course include:

- investment versus non-investment related cross-border business activities;
- the historical development and present significance of international greenfield and M&A activities;
- different forms of investment vehicles from a comparative perspective;
- domestic and public international law sources of investment law;
- investment restrictions;
- cross-border investment and corruption;
- structuring investment projects;
- due diligence;
- contract issues (including pre-signing arrangements, reps and warranties, disclosure letters);

[2]The LIBT I and II themes are now covered by Wolff 2013.

[3]Compare for initiatives to improve the education of future transactional lawyers Illig., pp. 221–222 and for the establishment of 'Transactional Practice Labs' to supplement doctrinal courses in 'Mergers & Acquisitions' and 'Real Estate Finance' at the University of Oregon, *ibid*, pp. 234–239.

- cross-border investment and technology transfer;
- labour issues;
- the taxation of cross-border investment projects; and
- China's investment regime as a case study.[4]

The main LIBT II themes are studied through in-class exercises, thus allowing students to gain the practical core skills that are necessary to deal with related issues in practice. These skills-based training modules include amongst others drafting, negotiation, presentation, and dispute settlement exercises. It is one of the key features of the LIBT II course that substantive law learning outcomes are acquired through legal skills training modules.

6.2.2 Delivery Mode

Like other postgraduate courses offered by the CUHK Faculty of Law the LIBT II course is conducted in the form of 13 teaching sessions per term with each teaching session consisting of three units of 45 min. In Term II of the academic year 2014–2015 when we have conducted our case study the LIBT II course was offered twice to cater to a double-intake of IEL students. LIBT II sessions were conducted during term time each Monday from 9:30 am to 12:15 pm and from 6:30 pm to 9:15 pm. Students were pre-assigned to attend only one of the two sessions to keep the class-size manageable.

No particular time is allocated to tutorials or other forms of small group teaching. The LIBT II skills training modules rather form part of 2.25 h LIBT II teaching sessions which in practice often extended to 2.5 h or even more.

The significance of interactivity in the classroom[5] and the importance of skills training not only at the vocational, but also at university level is nowadays widely acknowledged.[6] For this purpose, the design of the LIBT II course emphasizes in-class interaction. Each LIBT II teaching session normally starts with a Q&A module[7] of 15 to 20 min on topics taught in the previous week followed by a lecture type module with additional interactive elements to convey substantive knowledge on different LIBT II topics. Skills training exercises are normally conducted during the second part of each LIBT II session after a break of up to 15 min. Between 1 and 1.25 h are normally allocated to this part. Usually one, but sometimes two skills training exercises are conducted during the second half of the teaching session. For the sake of variation in some instances students are asked to work on very

[4]Also compare Wolff, 2013, pp. 275–430.

[5]Henriss-Anderssen; also compare in more detail *infra*, 6.2.4.

[6]For different approaches towards skills training see *e.g.* Wolski; Illig.

[7]For the 'traditional Socratic dialogue in the context of legal writing courses' see Atlas et al. pp. 46–48; *supra*, 3.4.

short skills training exercises at the beginning of a weekly LIBT II session as replacement of the Q&A session.

All skills training exercises are followed by in-class de-briefings during which students present their ‘products’ and feedback is given by other students and by the course teacher.[8] Also, on many occasions additional samples e.g. in the form of draft clauses or structuring models that had been used in practice are presented for benchmarking purposes.[9] In this regard students’ eagerness to ‘take home perfect models’ and the risk that these models might simply be copied without reflection has to be addressed.[10] In most cases this is done by presenting samples or models which are flawed in one (obvious) way or another as explained during the de-briefing discussion.

Finally, during the de-briefing discussions the purpose of the exercise is laid out in more detail and the ‘real case-nexus’ is established where possible by way of explanations how the particular case had developed in practice.

6.2.3 Hong Kong Specifics

Hong Kong’s postgraduate law student body is often diverse in terms of culture,[11] educational background, maturity, professional experience as well as English language skills.[12] This is particularly true for the IEL programme as it attracts students from all over the world and from all walks of life. Furthermore, many Asian LIBT II students are not used to interactive learning,[13] but have in the past rather been exposed only to the traditional lecture-type teaching mode.[14] Also, as already mentioned, CUHK postgraduate law courses are taught in the form of three hour sessions without small group components. The number of students per LIBT II class usually ranges between 65 and 85.

All these factors had to be considered for the design of the LIBT II course and are at the same time reasons for considering the flipping of the lecture modules as explained below.[15]

[8]On de-briefing sessions see McCormack/Simpson, pp. 75–76; Tyler/Cukier, p. 73; Webb/Maugham/Maugham/Keppel-Palmer/Boon, p. 2; Wolski, p. 294.

[9]For the educational benefits of analogical reasoning compare Tyler/Cukier, p. 76.

[10]Compare Harris/Susman, p. 200.

[11]For multicultural issues in legal education see O’Donnell.

[12]For a general discussion of possible responses to student diversity in legal education see Stevens/Douglas/Cullen-Mandikos/Hunter.

[13]Compare Freeland/Li/Young, pp. 225, 236.

[14]For the resultant ‘surface approach’, Henriss-Anderssen, p. 183.

[15]*Infra*, 6.3.

6.2.4 Pedagogical Underpinning

As mentioned,[16] the LIBT II course is enriched with in-class exercises designed to teach students practical core skills, such as contract drafting, negotiation, presentation and dispute settlement. The skills training was made an important component of the LIBT II course for a range of reasons. Students' active involvement in skills training exercises encourages them to apply and thus reflect and actively engage with substantive law themes provided that the skills training modules are designed accordingly.[17] The use of skills trainings is therefore in line with active learning theories which emphasizes that students learn best when they talk or write about what they learn and 'make what they learn part of themselves'.[18] The in-class exercises also offer opportunities for student-faculty interaction, a forum for peer support and the creation of a learning community. Furthermore the drafting and negotiation trainings give students the opportunity to exercise writing, oral and aural skills, mirroring the practice in a law firm.

The skills training exercises consequently reinforce the cognitive learning outcomes of the lecture modules. Vice versa the lecture modules supplement the affective and performative learning[19] during the skills training exercises. This is in acknowledgement that simulations alone are not effective teaching tools without being supplemented by other teaching activities.[20]

The LIBT II course has been well received by CUHK's postgraduate students in the past. Teaching evaluation indicated that students placed importance on the lecture module as it helps their understanding of the legal context. Practical examples used by the teacher to explain substantive law topics were regarded as particularly valuable as they provide clarifications to the black-letter content. This is not surprising as the real case scenarios used in the LIBT II context were meant to generate credibility and thus acceptance from the students' perspective.

Based on in-class observations and informal discussions with students, it has also become clear that students enjoyed and appreciated the interactive LIBT II modules. In particular, the skills training exercises encourage them to take a more active role thus facilitating the engagement with related substantive law concepts with sustainable results.[21] Most LIBT II students have never conducted any real (or simulated) practical work in the area of international business law. The skills training exercises meet their eagerness to explore something new. Students seem to value the fact that the LIBT II skills training exercises were designed as (simulated)

[16] *Supra*, 6.2.1.

[17] For similar observations made during a writing course see Hasche, pp. 267–294.

[18] Chickering/Gamson, in Seven Principles for Good Practice in Undergraduate Education.

[19] Compare McCormack/Simpson, p. 80; Henriss-Anderssen, p. 185; Kift, p. 46.

[20] Compare Tyler/Cukier, p. 68.

[21] Compare McCormack/Simpson, p. 66; Harris/Susman, p. 202; Wilcox, p. 449.

real case scenarios.[22] They appear to feel that this prepares them for what they are studying for, i.e. to work in the arena of international business law.[23] In fact, feedback received from former LIBT II students also confirms the usefulness of their learning experience for their later work as practicing lawyers.

6.3 Why 'Flipping' LIBT II Lecture Modules?

While the interactive LIBT II skills training modules were well received by students in the past, they faced some practical difficulties arising out of the large LIBT II class sizes and the fact that LIBT II classes are conducted in one lecture theatre without access e.g. to different breakout rooms.[24] Students therefore had to do group work and meet with other groups e.g. for negotiation purposes, in different corners of that very same lecture venue.

The large student number led to difficulties also during the de-briefing modules conducted after in-class exercises. In particular, time was hardly ever sufficient to give appropriate individual feedback.[25] Where students were requested to produce output in the written form it could be considered to provide feedback after class e.g. by email or via an online teaching platform. The obvious disadvantage of this approach—apart from the unrealistic demand on the time of the teacher[26]—is that written feedback is static and therefore a less effective teaching tool compared with any interactive mode.

For all these reasons it appeared to be sensible to consider 'flipping' the LIBT II lecture modules. As explained above,[27] lecturing occupied a major portion of the time of the weekly LIBT II sessions. It would be the main purpose of flipping the LIBT II lecture modules to free up more class time for exercises, in particular to allow for adequate feedback possibilities during the debriefings. Students would acquire the required basic knowledge of the related substantive law concepts before class via online lectures thus being in a position to engage in interactive and reflective in-class exercises. In other words, by flipping the LIBT II classroom, in-class time could be used more efficiently by concentrating on higher-order learning activities, such as application, analysis, synthesis and evaluation during face-to-face teacher-student time. In contrast, the lower-order learning activities such as knowledge acquisition and comprehension would be moved outside classroom.[28]

---

[22]*Supra*, 6.2.2.

[23]Compare from the legal writing point of view Wilcox, p. 449.

[24]*Infra*, 6.4.

[25]Compare McCormack/Simpson, p. 76; Wolski, pp. 291, 294; generally Hativa.

[26]Compare Hasche, p. 285.

[27]*Supra*, 6.2.2.

[28]*Supra*, 3.3.8.

The working hypothesis underpinning our case study therefore was, that flipping the LIBT II lecture modules would enhance the course to be delivered 'in the best balance of active and engaging face-to-face and online learning experience.'[29] Furthermore, our literature review suggested that the Flipped Classroom model is in line with a number of pedagogical theories.[30] We consequently anticipated that flipping the LIBT II lecture modules would generate the pedagogical benefits claimed by those theories.

6.4 Developing 'Flipped' LIBT II Classrooms

6.4.1 Pilot Scheme

While assuming that flipping all LIBT II lecture modules would possibly be best to achieve the benefits described above,[31] we also had to acknowledge our lack of experience and resources to do so. We also felt that it would be unfair to students to flip the entire LIBT II course at once and thus putting their whole LIBT II learning experience at risk in the case that the Flipped Classroom concept would not work in the LIBT II context.

We therefore concluded that it would be best to start small[32] by conducting a pilot project first. Instead of flipping the lecture modules of all the LIBTI II sessions, we decided to flip only two sessions. On the basis of the experience gained from the pilot project we would then decide to use the Flipped Classroom concept in a larger LIBT II context in the coming years. We saw another potential advantage of not flipping all of the lecture modules immediately in the fact that this would allow a comparison between teaching sessions delivered in the traditional way and those which were flipped.[33]

6.4.2 Selecting Sessions for 'Flipping'

Selecting the appropriate sessions for our pilot project was no easy task. First of all, to make use of skills training modules for substantive law learning purposes all LIBT skills training modules had been especially designed to align with particular, pre-determined substantive law learning outcomes. When designing the original

---

[29]Graham, pp. 3–21.

[30]Compare in particular, *supra* Chap. 3.

[31]*Supra*, 3.3.

[32]Compare Upchurch, p. 5.

[33]Compare *infra*, 6.5; Upchurch, p. 5.

LIBT courses it therefore had to be decided (i) which substantive law topics should be covered and, and (ii) which skills should be used for particular modules.

Second, the selection of the two sessions for the pilot project had to ensure that the topics selected had to be suitable for 'flipping'. Initially, we had planned to flip the lecture modules of the sessions covering three topics, namely 'due diligence', 'private international investment law' and 'contract drafting' for the following reasons:

According to past teaching experience these topics are relatively straight forward and we anticipated that students would not have problems to acquire the related substantive knowledge via online lectures. Furthermore, the lecture contents of the sessions covering these topics are of moderate length and could therefore be easily contained in 30-min online lectures. In addition, the in-class exercises related to these topics often produced multiple answers varying according to cultural backgrounds, leading to intensive and prolonged discussions. Extra in-class time therefore seemed especially useful to ensure adequate time for feedback, discussion and de-briefing.

However, eventually, we decided to flip the lecture modules of two sessions covering other topics instead, namely 'Case Study: Mainland China's Investment Law System (1)' and 'Case Study: Mainland China's Investment Law System (2)'. This decision was based on three main reasons. First, these two topics are taught towards the end of the course when teacher and students are already rather familiar with each other which should facilitate communications regarding the Flipped Classroom concept. Second, the in-class exercises related to these sessions are more comprehensive as they involve a combination of the legal skills which students should have learnt throughout the entire course. The in-class exercises of these two sessions therefore require more time to complete which led to problems related to time constraints in the past. By 'flipping' the lecture modules of the two selected teaching sessions more time would become available to engage in the in-class exercises. Third, a PowerPoint presentation for both sessions had been updated and tested recently for other purposes and were readily available. We therefore had to expect that flipping the lecture modules of the chosen topics would reduce the preparation time and efforts substantially. Last but not least, since the topics had been presented recently in another context the teacher could build on this experience when preparing the online lecture and thus improve the quality of the online lectures.

6.4.3 *'White Board Approach', 'Screen Capture Approach', 'Audio-Only Format' or OERs?*

As discussed above, there are three common ways to create 'flipped lectures', i.e. the 'white board approach', the 'screen capture approach' and the 'audio-only format'.[34] For the decision which of these ways would be most appropriate for the

[34]*Supra*, 4.3.

purpose of our LIBT II pilot project, we had to acknowledge that we lacked any relevant technical expertise, we did not have the necessary pedagogical experience, there was a shortage of manpower and finally we had budgetary constraints. The audio approach, therefore would have been the rational choice. However, we found that a recording application called Echo 360[35] was available at our University. Echo 360 was said to provide easy solutions to the 'screen capture approach' and has a reputation for being very user-friendly. In fact, some experience within the Faculty of Law with Echo 360 suggested this to be correct. For verification purposes an additional trial recording was carried out by one of the authors using an Echo 360 pre-installed computer in the Faculty IT Department office in November 2014. The trial confirmed that the Echo 360 application is easy to use and provides simple editing tools. We consequently decided to use Echo 360 and to adopt the 'screen capture approach' instead of just doing audio recording.

For the sake of completeness it must be mentioned, that we have also considered using OERs rather than to make our own videos from scratch. However, our initial research suggested that it is impossible to locate 'suitable' OERs for teaching any of the LIBT II topics as further explained below.[36]

6.4.4 In Particular: Echo 360

Echo 360 is an 'active learning platform' and was introduced to our University by the CUHK Centre for Learning and Enhancing and Research (CLEAR). Echo 360[37] is an all-in-one media system that allows teachers to record their lectures, embed online learning activities, store teaching materials and keep statistics of students' performance.[38] Echo 360 was launched at our University during the time when the Occupy Central movement took to the streets in Hong Kong. It was used to record lectures to make up for classes which had to be cancelled during the first week of October 2014 as a result of the movement. Furthermore, Echo 360 is currently also used within our University for lecture capture purposes i.e. to record lectures for later review by students online.

For the development of Flipped Classrooms, Echo 360 can be used to deliver the 'white board approach', 'screen capture approach' or the 'audio-only format'. Under the 'screen capture approach',[39] Echo 360 is first installed onto a personal computer. When Echo 360 is activated the teacher can 'play' a PowerPoint

---

[35] *Infra*, 6.4.4.

[36] *Infra*, 6.4.5.

[37] Echo 360 active learning, Echo 360 website. http://echo360.com/ (last visited on 25 August 2015).

[38] *Ibid.*

[39] Compare *supra*, 4.3.3.

presentation on the same computer and start ‘lecturing’. The software will combine the movement of the presentation with the teacher’s voice. The teacher can control the lecturing by simply pressing the ‘play’ and ‘stop’ buttons on the computer.

Echo 360 also allows some editing after the recording is completed. This could involve removing background noise (if necessary), checking of the visual and audio quality to see if a second recording is necessary, arranging the recorded lectures in a particular sequence, naming of the lectures, removing parts which are deemed unnecessary and dividing recordings into several mini-lectures.

Adopting the ‘white board approach’ under Echo 360 is slightly more complicated than using the ‘screen capture approach’ as the visual image of the teacher would have to be recorded through a camera pre-installed in a classroom. Before recording, the personal computer (with Echo 360 pre-installed) has to be linked to the video recording system of the classroom. The ‘white board approach’ is therefore only viable under Echo 360 if a classroom with a video recording system is available. The recording of audio-only format is similar to that of ‘screen capture approach’, but without the visual presentation.

6.4.5 In Particular: Searching for LIBT II Compatible OERs

6.4.5.1 General

As explained above,[40] for a number of reasons it may be advantageous to rely on OERs rather than to develop Flipped Classrooms from scratch. This section reports on our difficulties to identify suitable OERs for flipping LIBT II lecture modules as planned.

6.4.5.2 Choice of Source

We had initially considered searching for OERs in YouTube EDU and podcasts (or iTunes U), the two largest repositories of educational videos. We then decided to rely on one source only, namely YouTube EDU. The main advantage of YouTube EDU as compared with podcasts is that for personal computer (non-Apple device) the podcast programme does not come with the computer, but has to be downloaded separately.[41] Even if students have downloaded iTunes successfully onto their own computers (other than Mac computers, iPads or iPhones) they must open iTunes on the apple website and run iTunes on a separate screen to be able to

---

[40]*Supra*, 5.4.

[41]iTunes website, Apple Inc. http://www.apple.com/itunes/ (last visited on 25 August 2015).

access podcasts.[42] This may be burdensome for students who use a non-Apple device.

6.4.5.3 The Experience of Searching for Suitable OERs

(1) Introduction

As already indicated, the process of searching for the OERs suitable for LIBT II purposes was much more difficult than first anticipated.

We were searching for OERs which ideally would allow students to watch one 10–30 min video that covers all the issues of a particular topic. And, we have given priority to videos produced and uploaded by universities, trade organizations and law firms over videos made by individuals to facilitate the checking for copyrights and credibility before use.

However, our search revealed that it is hardly possible to find videos that meet these two criteria in relation to those topics which we had identified for 'flipping' purposes.[43] While videos available online do not cover all aspects relevant for the different LIBT II topics, they normally contain at the same time much irrelevant information. For example, 'conflict of laws' does normally not refer to investment related aspects as covered in the LIBT II context. Instead available videos on 'conflict of laws' may refer to areas like contract law, family law or land law. Similar problems arose when searching for videos on 'international investment law'. Most videos put importance on policy issues or recent trends rather than on the transactional aspects. In fact, videos on the transactional aspects of cross-border investment law are not as common at all.

It was also difficult to find videos which offer the required depth. Some videos are book reviews or (teaser-) introductions to a course offered at a university. Other videos are recordings of seminars or commentaries on case studies and thus too specific for students with no background knowledge.

For some of the OERs which we have considered the audio recording was either not good enough or the speaker speaks with a particular accent that makes the video contents difficult to understand. Though YouTube provides English subtitles, since the subtitles are produced automatically by software and unchecked, mistakes are common, potentially leading to even more confusion than without the subtitles.

Because the suitability of each video had to be assessed one by one for each topic we had to watch more than 30 videos before something remotely useful was found. The process was time-consuming and frustrating.

OERs which have been identified for the topics due diligence, contract drafting skills, conflict of investment laws and Mainland Chinese investment law system are

---

[42] *Ibid.*

[43] *Supra*, 6.4.2.

set out in Appendix C.2. Some additional topic-specific information is provided in the following sections to demonstrate the difficulties encountered.

(2) Topic: due diligence

OERs addressing due diligence should cover the following issues:

- definition,
- goals,
- stages,
- due diligence report,
- practical difficulties,
- representations and warranties, and
- disclosure letters.

Our search revealed that YouTube is not short of videos on due diligence. However, in most of the videos, due diligence is addressed from a wide angle with focus on the definition, purpose and different types of due diligence. It was difficult to locate an OER with focus on due diligence in the cross-border M&A context.

(3) Topic: contract drafting

OERs addressing contract drafting should for LIBT II purposes cover the following issues:

- purpose,
- guiding principles (such as using plain language, avoidance of redundancies, consistency, appropriate wording, avoidance of ambiguities),
- layout,
- numbering, articles, sections,
- headers,
- punctuations, and
- the use of the active vs passive voice.

The search for appropriate 'contract drafting videos' was even more time-consuming than the search for due diligence related OERs. About 20 videos on 'contract drafting' and 'contract drafting skills' have been viewed. Many of these address which contract terms have to be included in a contract. However, none of the videos which we were able to locate deals with cross-border investment contracts. In other words, there are only very limited OERs which are usable for the purpose of flipping the LIBT II lecture module on contract drafting.

(4) Topic: conflict of (investment) laws

OERs on conflict of (investment) laws should cover the following issues:

- sources of investment law,
- conflict of laws in general,
- special conflicts rules and principles related to investment projects.

The search for suitable videos covering the topic 'conflict of (investment) laws' was by far the most challenging task. Again, we had to conclude that conflicts-related OERs for LIBT II purposes are not readily available.

(5) Topic: Mainland China's Investment Law System (1) & (2)

OERs on Mainland China's investment law system should cover the following issues:

- due diligence in China,
- the law governing M&A transactions and government control,
- structuring options,
- acquisition of FIE equity interest,
- foreign investors acquiring equity interest in non-FIE Chinese companies,
- asset deals conducted by foreign investors,
- onshore acquisitions,
- mergers,
- industry-specific M&A regulations,
- offshore special purpose vehicles, outbound M&As and round-trip investments,
- the Draft Foreign Investment Law.

No OER identified online was sufficiently comprehensive to cover all these topics with the required depth. The reason may be that Mainland China's investment law system is fast-changing with a vast amount of information becoming available almost on a daily basis. Covering the above topics in OERs requires specific and extensive knowledge which makes the task even more challenging than conventional OERs with the risk to be outdated soon after they are produced.

(6) Conclusions

The LIBT II course does not follow standard patterns. In its current form it is unique and not offered by other institutions. It is therefore not very surprising that OERs are not readily available online. In fact, the more unique a course is the more difficult it will it be to locate suitable OERs. In contrast, our cursory online search has revealed that for standard law course topics, such as e.g. contract law and torts, much more OER variety is available online.

6.4.6 Distribution

6.4.6.1 General

For students to fully engage in the Flipped Classroom model, the distribution platform must allow the video/audio lectures to be (1) easily accessible and (2) user-friendly. For the purposes of our pilot project we had to choose between two available options which meet both criteria, i.e. the Blackboard online learning platform and podcasts.

6.4.6.2 The Blackboard Approach

The major benefit of using Blackboard for distribution is that LIBT II students are already familiar with it as Blackboard is widely used for disseminating teaching materials in our university. Using Blackboard for distributing the audio files allows students access with one password and little additional technical work would be necessary for the distribution of the online lectures. Storage under Blackboard can ensure that video lectures are protected against any unauthorized use by other parties. In addition, our university's IT team had explained the following:

- Even though the technology 'streaming' is not available in Blackboard, a similar technology called 'progressive download' can ensure that video lectures are ready for viewing when the file is viewed progressively.
- One advantage of using Echo 360 is that since it is linked to Blackboard, the recording could be distributed to students by pressing the 'upload' button. Echo 360 will format the recording and this may only take up to 2–4 h depending on the length and size of the recording. After that, students could access the recording via Blackboard.
- For the development of more sophisticated Flipped Classroom projects, we could rely on assistance from an e-learning team formed by our University to assist teachers with related activities.

6.4.6.3 The Podcast Approach

We have discussed podcasting as a tool to distribute Flipped Classrooms in an earlier chapter.[44] The main advantage of podcasting lies in its popularity. We had to consider it to be likely that LIBT II students were already familiar with this technology and access to podcasts would require little technical support. Since streaming is embedded in podcasting, it allows instant enjoyment to the audio file while at the same time downloading it. However, podcasting means that course materials and audio files are stored separately. We saw the risk that students might feel overloaded when accessing podcasting. In addition, podcasting makes the audio file publicly accessible and the distribution can therefore not be controlled. Though there are plenty of websites that offer step-by-step instructions to set up podcasts on the Internet and YouTube, the technology required for podcasting is relatively complicated and involves technologies such as transforming MP3 file into a podcasting compatible format and encoding an RSS Feed. It therefore appeared necessary to engage the help of experts when using the podcasting technology. Given these difficulties and the advantages of the Blackboard approach we decided that distribution via Blackboard was preferable.

[44]*Supra*, 2.2.3.

6.4.7 The Recording Process

A total of eight videos were produced in the beginning of March 2015. A ninth video, a public lecture by one of the authors recorded earlier in January 2015, was also recommended to be viewed by students in preparation of the two flipped LIBT II sessions. The nine videos together have a total length of 230 min. The shortest one is about nine and the longest about 53 min long. For the reasons explained above, the eight videos were produced in a 'screen capture approach',[45] using the Echo 360 programme[46] pre-installed on a University laptop computer. The eight newly produced videos were uploaded to the University Blackboard system.[47] Students were informed about the ninth video which is available online at University website via the lecture materials.

The recording was carried out in the teacher's office who simply delivered the lecture to the laptop computer. A research assistant did some simple editing to improve the sound quality and an IT engineer was on stand-by to give technical advice. In total four hours were spent on the recording, editing and developing and sending instructions to Echo 360 to upload the videos.

The whole process was much easier and less burdensome than we had expected. Apart from a minor technical hip-cup in the first hour of recording, all eight recordings were made in one-go without any difficulty. Having said that, the teacher found that face-to-face lecturing is much easier than video recording a lecture. This is because in a face-to-face lecture the teacher can see students' reactions, test their understanding and make additional explanations and corrections when deemed necessary. When video recording lectures these options do obviously not exist. In contrast, subject to the possibility of minor editorial changes later, the teacher has to deliver his lecture 'ready-for-consumption' which requires a high level of preparation and concentration.

6.4.8 Preparing for the LIBT II for the Flipped Classroom Experience

To gain full cooperation from students the teacher spent a significant amount of time in the week before to 'flipped' LIBT II sessions to introduce the Flipped Classroom model to students.[48] Students seemed to be appreciative and also excited about the new learning experience.

---

[45]*Supra*, 4.3.3 and 6.4.3.

[46]*Supra*, 6.4.4.

[47]*Supra*, 6.4.6.2.

[48]For communication needs see *supra*, 3.6.4.4.

Our trial Flipped Classrooms related to the tenth and eleventh sessions of the second semester of 2014/15 academic year. The video lectures were uploaded during the week of the ninth session to allow students sufficient time for viewing. An additional announcement of the changed teaching pattern in weeks 10 and 11 and a video list[49] were uploaded to Blackboard to remind students of the importance of viewing the video lectures before coming to class. Furthermore, also reading suggestions[50] were provided via Blackboard to allow students who prefer reading over watching video lectures to prepare for the two flipped sessions.

6.5 Evaluation

6.5.1 Developing an Evaluation Framework

6.5.1.1 General

The success of the two LIBT II Flipped Classrooms must be benchmarked against the educational goals of their introduction. We consequently had to assess if students appreciate the (new) learning experience as a result of the introduction of the Flipped Classroom concept and if this ultimately also improves the learning outcomes. Can and do students in fact acquire the same level of knowledge when the lecture module is ‘flipped’ and thus moved outside the classroom? Are the learning outcomes more sustainable when being reinforced by more in-class interactivity? Are students’ practical skills improved by the extra time for in-class exercises?

6.5.1.2 Measuring the Learning Experience

The difficulty associated with the evaluation of students’ learning experience in the LIBT II Flipped Classroom project was to identify a measurable definition of the quality of interaction. Learning experience is often varied by multiple factors, such as the course topic, the course content, the delivery time, the learning atmosphere, students’ own expectation as well as interest and personal experience in the subject of teacher and students.[51]

Acknowledging these challenges we have used four main evaluation tools. First, we have collected data (generated by the Echo 360 system[52]) to verify how many students have watched the online videos at what time. Second, we have tried to

---

[49]*Infra*, Appendix C.2.

[50]Infra, 3.3.

[51]Compare Dziuban/Moskal, p. 238.

[52]Compare *infra*, 6.5.2.2.

observe (through an independent third party) students' behavior during those sessions which as a result of the 'flipping' of the lecture modules were entirely devoted to interactive modules.[53] Third, we have developed a questionnaire[54] (the Questionnaire) to be completed by students at the end of the course. The focus of the Questionnaire was on the comparison of their Flipped Classroom experience with their experience of traditional classroom lecture modules. Following the model of others[55] we have divided the Questionnaire into five parts covering the following topics[56]:

- Part I—User experience relating to the contents of the video lectures:
  Questions explore whether students find the Flipped Classroom arrangement (more) flexible, their learning habits and their purpose of usage, and whether students prefer face-to-face or video instead.
- Part II—User experience relating to in-class interaction:
  Questions aim to identify those components students appreciate in an interactive classroom.
- Part III—User experience relating to the quality of the video files:
  Questions address the visual and audio quality of the video lectures, the adequacy of the lecture pace and the downloading speed as well as whether students find the video lectures easily accessible.
- Part IV—User experience relating to the technical support:
  Questions ask about technical problems students have encountered and whether they were satisfied with the technical support.
- Part V—User resistance:
  In case students did not use the video lectures at all, questions in this part attempt to explore the reasons.

Finally, as a fourth evaluation tool, we have compared the course and teaching evaluations of the LIBT II course with two 'flipped' lecture modules with those of past years when the traditional delivery mode had been adopted.

For the whole evaluation exercise, it had to be kept in mind that students tend to pay more attention to the overall experience and less to individual aspects of a course identified in a questionnaire.[57] Moreover, the possibility that students seldom consider the course mode an important element when grading their educational experience had to be factored in.[58] Finally, under the pilot scheme, we have only

---

[53]*Infra*, 6.5.2.3.

[54]Appendices C.4 and C.5.

[55]Work which we have consulted for designing the questionnaire include Beck; Davis/Neary/Vaughn; Gerdy/Wise/Craig; Lemmer; Lihosit/Larrington; McKellar/Maharg; Upchurch. Note, however, that these authors did not publish their questionnaires in the articles quoted.

[56]Compare *infra*, Appendices C.4 and C.5.

[57]Dziuban/Moskal, p. 239.

[58]*Ibid.*

flipped two topics and we have to acknowledge that students may benchmark their learning experience in relation to these topics against other topics rather than against the mode of delivery of the other LIBT II sessions. In other words, we are aware that the findings of our comparative evaluation of learning experiences may not represent the ultimate truth. However, we are confident that they can be seen as an indication which allows for forward-looking decisions in relation to research on and the actual application of the Flipped Classroom concept.

6.5.1.3 Measuring Learning Outcomes

The precise evaluation of learning outcomes of Flipped Classrooms is challenging mainly for two reasons.[59] First, it is often difficult to isolate the variable, i.e. the 'flipped' lecture, from other modules of a teaching session in the process of evaluation. Second, a diverse student body may lead to very different assumptions and perceptions in relation to particular aspects of a course.[60]

Ideally, to assess the learning outcomes of the LIBT II Flipped Classroom approach the end-of-term examination results should have been compared with those of previous years when no parts of the LIBT II sessions were flipped. As a matter of Faculty policy we are, however, not able to use the same or even similar exam questions twice. Exam questions consequently have to differ substantially each year. Furthermore, the LIBT II student body changes from year to year with e.g. a greater portion of part-time students having registered in the year when the LIBT II Flipped Classroom pilot scheme was conducted. In addition, improved academic performance, if any, may be attributable to an increase in time spent on learning by a particular year's student cohort, rather than to the new course design. Grades may also fluctuate according each year's intake quality. In any event, good students do normally well in any mode.[61]

Due to all these difficulties we had to conclude that the comparison of examination results of different LIBT II cohorts could not generate reliable results. We have consequently opted not to engage this comparative evaluation method. However, we intend to explore this option further in the future with the ultimate goal to develop an appropriate comparative evaluation methodology with control and treatment groups and pre-and post-tests.[62]

---

[59]Compare Ginns/Ellis, p. 54.

[60]Compare Le Brun/Johnstone, p. 69.

[61]Dziuban/Moskal, p. 240.

[62]Sharpe/Benfield/Roberts/Francis, pp. 50–51.

6.5.2 *Evaluating the LIBT II Pilot Scheme*

6.5.2.1 General

In the previous sections we have explained how we have flipped lecture modules in the LIBT II context and what has guided us when evaluating the success of the LIBT II Flipped Classrooms. This section now reports on the outcome of our evaluation exercise.

6.5.2.2 Statistics Generated by Echo 360

The Flipped Classroom concept requires students to contribute extra time for viewing the video lectures prior to coming to class. According to our past experience, however, Hong Kong students invest only very limited time on the preparation for lectures.[63] Despite the basic assumption underlying this study, i.e. that students find online lectures engaging and inspiring, we were consequently in doubt if Flipped Classrooms could work in Hong Kong. Statistics as to how many students have viewed the online lectures have eased these doubts only to a certain extent.

Appendix C.6 sets out the detailed numbers of LIBT II students who have visited the LIBT II online lectures at different points of times. We have collected the numbers separately for the respective videos relating to Week 10 and to Week 11 at two different times on the day the respective in-class sessions took place, i.e. prior to the morning session and prior to the evening session. To understand if additional students have watched the online videos after the concerned LIBT II session, but before the examination we have also collected viewer numbers on the day after the examination.

Out of 138 students (only) between 94/86 students of the morning LIBT II sessions and 73/67 students of the evening sessions have watched the four videos relating to the week 10/11 sessions respectively prior to class. Additional students have watched the videos after class, but prior to the examination. The average number of students viewing each video lecture prior to class is, however, not more than 73 for week 10 and 68 for week 11. We found these numbers disappointingly low.

The most popular of the video lectures was the first one of the tenth session (100 viewers) on 'Mainland China's Investment Law System—Introduction'. The least viewed one was the last video lecture of the eleventh session (77 viewers) on 'Labour Issue'. The reason for the different viewing rates is unclear. One possible explanation could be that the level of enthusiasm for students to view video lectures

[63] In contrast, at least in the LIBT II context students did seem to engage rather intensively in follow-up studies and thus in preparations for the Q&A sessions at the beginning of each LIBT teaching session.

dropped the more video lectures have been viewed. An alternative explanation is that students could not find the time to view all of the video lectures and concentrated on the first.

The least viewed video lectures was also the shortest one (only 9 min). Interestingly this contradicts the common understanding that students prefer shorter video lectures.[64]

Data generated by Echo 360 also show that all videos were viewed by some of the students more than once. The average cumulative viewing is 1.6. i.e. the video lectures were viewed on average 1.6 times per viewer. The highest cumulatively viewed video lecture is the first video of the eleventh session on M&A in China, reaching an average cumulative viewing rate of 2.4. This can be explained with the complexity of the topic which covers difficult issues such as the comparison of different M&A methods in China. The least cumulatively viewed video lecture is the last of the eleventh session on 'Labour issues', reaching only an average cumulative viewing rate of 1.2. Since this video covers straight forward contents, it can be assumed that students did not see the need to view it multiple times as the contents are easy to understand.

The average completion rate for all video lectures was 89 %. Average completion rate means the percentage of video lectures students complete in one viewing. The relatively high percentage means that overall students manage to complete viewing the video lectures without quitting in the middle. This is also an encouraging indication that the video lectures are engaging.

6.5.2.3 In-Class Observations

It is one purpose of the Flipped Classroom concept to provide free up time for students to engage in in-class exercises. In the tenth session, three individual and one group exercises and in the eleventh session, one individual and two group exercises were offered to students. This compared favorably with the traditional LIBT II teaching model used in previous years, where there was normally only time for one in-class exercise.

About 65–70 students attended the tenth and eleventh morning sessions, indicating little change in the attendance rate compared to previous sessions. In both sessions, during the first part an interactive Q&A session was conducted to test students' understanding of the topics. The debriefing was to some extent a repetition of some parts of the video contents. The teacher also added explanations by using examples presented in in-class exercises of previous sessions to help students grasp the bigger picture.

During debriefings, some students were seen jotting down notes but others merely listened. The reason for not taking notes was unclear—whether it was

[64] *Supra*, 6.5.2.4.

because they have viewed the videos beforehand and were familiar with the contents or because they simply did not have a habit of taking notes.

The level of attention increased whenever the teacher asked students tricky questions or when no student got the answer right. During the debriefing of a contract drafting exercises, students were most enthusiastic to learn how to improve their own answers. In general students seemed to enjoy group exercise. Some of them were actively involved in the discussions, but some merely observed with little participation.

There were no in-class observations which related specifically to the Flipped Classroom model. In other words, in-class observations did not help to understand whether the adoption of the Flipped Classroom model improved the learning experience and the learning outcomes except possibly that no open objection to the chosen teaching mode was voiced in class.

6.5.2.4 Student Feedback

(1) Background

During the last LIBT II session, students were asked to complete the Questionnaire. A total number of 125 (of a total student number of 138) students participated in the questionnaire. 81.6 % were full-time and 18.4 % were part-time students. The majority of students (92.8 %) were either Mainland Chinese (68 %) or Hong Kong students (24.8 %). There were only seven students from other areas. 96.8 % of the students replied that they have watched at least one video lecture once before or after class. This figure is surprisingly high and not explainable given the above data generated via Echo 360 regarding the number of viewers.[65] One possible explanation might be the difference between the way questions were designed in the Questionnaire and how data were recorded by Echo 360. The Questionnaire asked students if they have watched 'at least one' video lecture while Echo 360 counted the viewing record according to the actual number of students having watched 'each' of the videos. If a certain number of students decided not to watch any more videos after having watched one, the Questionnaire would produce a positive answer but Echo 360 would record only one count of view for the one video lecture but null for the rest.

40 students said that they liked one or more of the video lectures provided in the tenth session. 23 students commented similarly on video lectures provided for the eleventh session. Seven students said they liked all video lectures.

(2) Flexible learning

Most of the students found that the video lectures allow flexible learning. 72.8 % of the students agreed or strongly agreed that the video lectures gave them flexibility

---

[65] *Supra*, 6.5.2.2.

when preparing for in-class sessions.[66] 80 % of the students replied that they had watched at least one video lecture before coming to class.[67] Again, this number needs to be considered with care given the data generated via the Echo 360 system.[68] 5.6 % replied that they have watched the videos also after class and another 8.8 % said that they watched both before and after class.[69] Most of the students (67.2 %) watched the video lectures at home, 11.2 % watched them at university and 8.8 % watched video lectures both at home and at university.[70]

(3) Video lectures help revision

77.6 % of the respondents found that the video lectures helped them understand the topics.[71] Although the video contents were produced based on the materials from the reading suggestions, 32.8 % of students still disagreed or strongly disagreed that they could understand the lecture topics by reading relevant materials alone (without watching the video lectures).[72] One student commented that video lectures are not as comprehensive as the face-to-face lectures.

65.6 % of the students indicated that they would use the video lectures for revision.[73] When asked whether they would watch all or some of the video lectures again before the examination, the number dropped to 48 %.[74] However, one student commented that he/she liked the video lectures because he/she could re-watch them.

(4) In-class interaction

In general, students seemed to value the in-class exercises. 75.2 % of the respondents disagreed or strongly disagreed with the statement that the use of video lectures allowed them to skip classes.[75] 50.4 % of the students confirmed that they liked video lectures because this allowed for more time for in-class exercises.[76] 51.2 % of the students replied that they enjoyed the in-class exercises in the tenth and eleventh sessions more than the exercises in other sessions.[77] 69.6 % stated that they have participated more actively in in-class exercises in the tenth and eleventh sessions than the other sessions.[78] However, two students provided additional

---

[66] Question 13, Part III (a).

[67] Question 1, Part III (b).

[68] *Supra*, 6.5.2.2.

[69] *Ibid.*

[70] Question 2, Part III (b).

[71] Question 11, Part III (a).

[72] Question 1, Part III (c).

[73] Question 12, Part III (a).

[74] Question 9, Part III (a).

[75] Question 14, Part III (a).

[76] Question 10, Part III (a).

[77] Question 2, Part III (c).

[78] Question 3, Part III (c).

comments to the extent that they found the time provided for discussion was too long and took away the focus.

(5) Comparison with face-to-face lectures

When asked to compare the experience between video lectures and face-to-face lectures, the answers are not coherent. 40 % of the respondents replied that they prefer to have more time for in-class exercises rather than spending in-class time listening to lectures.[79] 34.4 % even said that they look forward to taking courses using video lectures in the future.[80] However, 54.4 % of the respondents indicated that they would choose face-to-face lectures instead of watching video lectures[81] and only 12.8 % would choose watching video lectures instead of face-to-face lectures.[82] The preference for face-to-face lectures is slightly higher for full-time students (55.9 %) than for part-time students (47.8 %). There is also a slight difference in preference between Chinese and non-Chinese students. More Chinese students (55.1 %) opted for face-to-face lectures than non-Chinese students (42.9 %), while the percentage of non-Chinese students who preferred video lectures (71.4 %) is higher than the percentage of Chinese students (55.1 %).

In the additional comment section, one student remarked that he/she thinks that it is a good idea to use video lectures to replace parts of the suggested readings and in-class exercises that require the knowledge covered by the video lectures motivate him/her to watch the video lectures before coming to class. Four students replied that they find face-to-face lectures more engaging than video lectures and that their level of concentration is higher in face-to-face lectures.

(6) Quality of video lectures

81.6 % of students indicated the video lectures were visually clear.[83] 88 % found that the audio quality of the video lectures was clear[84] and that the content was delivered at an appropriate speed (84.8 %).[85] 88 % of students agreed or strongly agreed that the teacher's presentation was clear.[86] 76.8 % agreed or strongly agreed that the video lectures were of the right length.[87] Contrary to this, 20 % of students replied that it was too-consuming to watch all the video lectures.[88] In the additional comment section, one respondent added that he/she was not motivated to watch any video longer than 20 min. Another student commented that he/she prefers short

[79] Question 4, Part III (c).
[80] Question 5, Part III (c).
[81] Question 7, Part III (a).
[82] Question 8, Part III (a).
[83] Question 1, Part III (a).
[84] Question 2, Part III (a).
[85] Question 4, Part III (a).
[86] Question 3, Part III (a).
[87] Question 6, Part III (a).
[88] Question 17, Part III (a).

videos to long ones and since there is nothing students cannot learn from reading, a simple introductory video would be sufficient. One part-time student responded that it is unrealistic to ask part-time students to find the time to watch the video lectures before coming to class. This response seems to correspond with the discussion of students' overload on which we have reported above.[89]

In relation to the format of the videos, six students commented in the additional comment section that they prefer to have the PowerPoint slides separately from the video lectures so that they had something to read while watching the video lectures. One student responded that he/she prefers the 'talking head', i.e. the white board approach,[90] to the screen capture approach.[91] Another commented that he/she prefers the audio-only format[92] with separate reading materials. Three students responded that the fonts used in the PowerPoint slides were too small for viewing.

(7) Technical issues

52 % of students did not experience any technical issues.[93] 24.8 % of students responded that they could watch, but not download the videos from Echo 360.[94] After investigation with our University IT team, we found that the 'download' function had been disabled intentionally to protect the copyrights related to the videos.

11.2 % of the students responded that their device was not compatible.[95] According to consultation with the Faculty IT team, we found that viewing of video lectures via Echo 360 should not cause any issue since viewing does not require specific software or browser.[96] One possible explanation for the presumed incompatibility problems was that on-going updates in browsers and integrated components (Java, Flash) may have caused viewing problems. Another possible explanation could be that the security setting in the students' computer restricted certain multimedia files from playing. A future solution for these problems therefore might be to advise students to upload more than one browser to their computer to circumvent this challenge.[97]

(8) Non-watchers

Only four students stated that they did not watch any of the video lectures at all. Again, according to the above Echo 360 data,[98] the total number is potentially much higher. One student explained that he/she did not know the importance of

---

[89] *Supra*, 3.6.5.

[90] *Supra*, 4.3.2.

[91] *Supra*, 4.3.3.

[92] *Supra*, 4.3.4.

[93] Question 1, Part IV (a).

[94] *Ibid.*

[95] *Ibid.*

[96] Compatible browsers include Internet Explorer, Firefox, Google Chrome and Safari.

[97] Slomanson, p. 102.

[98] *Supra*, 6.5.2.2.

watching video lectures.[99] Three students commented that they either did not know how to watch or download the video lectures or they could not find time to watch the video lectures.[100]

6.5.2.5 Course and Teaching Evaluations

Course and teaching evaluations (CTE) in relation to the LIBT II course were part of the university-wide CTE exercise. This exercise is conducted for all undergraduate courses and most postgraduate courses during the last two weeks of all terms each year. It takes the form of online questionnaires containing 18 statements which students have to rate from (1) (disagree) to (5) (strongly agree) in relation to the evaluated course.

For the evaluation of our pilot project we have compared this year's CTE scores with the scores of the past two years when LIBT II was delivered entirely in the traditional mode, i.e. without 'flipping'. Furthermore, we have compared three of the 18 statements of previous years with the statements of the year when LIBT II sessions were 'flipped'. These statements ask students to give scores in relation to: 'Supported by IT resources', 'Satisfaction with course' and 'Satisfaction with teacher'. The CTE questionnaire allows students to make additional qualitative comments and we were interested to learn if any student had commented on the 'flipped' modules.

It is obvious that the CTE scores comparison has its limits and cannot be taken as absolute truth. First, each year's student body is different in terms of intake quality, national and cultural background, work-experience and full-time vs part-time status. In addition, in the year when the pilot scheme was conducted the course teacher had—unlike in previous years—not also taught the LIBT I course. This may have affected students' view on the LIBT II course. For example, students with lower grades in the LIBT I course are likely to give the teacher lower teaching scores for the LIBT II course. And, students who have familiarized themselves with the teacher's teaching style during the LIBT I course may have looked at the LIBT II course more favorably. Moreover, in 2012/13 the LIBT II course was only offered once, whereas in 2013/14 and 2014/15 due to a double intake the LIBT II course was taught twice on the same day for different groups of students, i.e. in a morning and in an evening session.[101] Finally, the CTE questionnaire used in 2012/13 differed slightly from the one used in the following two years in form and substance. For example, it had asked students to confirm agreement with full statements, i.e. 'The course was well supported by library resources', 'Overall, I am satisfied with the course.' and 'Overall, I am satisfied with the teacher …'s

[99]Question 2, Part II.

[100]Question 3 and 4, Part III.

[101]The morning session was delivered from 9:30am to 12:15 pm and the evening session from 6:30 pm to 9:15 pm.

performance.' Despite all these problems regarding the empirical reliability of the data collected we feel that they can give at least an indication how students felt about in the introduction of Flipped Classrooms in the LIBT II context.

The LIBT II 2012/13, 2013/14 and 2014/15 CTE raw scores[102] were as follows:

Academic year	2012/13		2013/14		2014/15	
Sessions	Morning	Evening	Morning	Evening	Morning	Evening
Response rate	Not available		65.67 %	50 %	59.72 %	40.30 %
Support by IT resources	5.35	n/a	5.16	5.23	5.40	5.56
Satisfaction with the course	5.57	n/a	5.35	5.47	5.65	5.56
Satisfaction with the teacher	5.73	n/a	5.33	5.53	5.84	5.78

Only one student made additional qualitative comments on the Flipped Classrooms. Due to the obvious time constraints in class the student welcomed the 'flipping' of some of the lecture modules, but suggested to 'flip' one additional week to be able to have one in-class exercise that combines the topics of different LITB II sessions.

The CTE scores were higher in the year when the pilot scheme was conducted than in the previous two years. As mentioned above, this has to be considered with great care as different reasons may have led to these higher scores.[103] However, it can be concluded that the use of Flipped Classrooms has at least not negatively affected students' perception of the course. This is also shown by the fact that no negative comments were received on the use of Flipped Classrooms.

As discussed above,[104] one of the reasons for teachers' resistance to adopt the Flipped Classroom model is the fact that this might affect their teaching evaluations. Our study suggests that this fear is unjustified although it must again be acknowledged that it is difficult to generalize the results of our study at this point of time.

6.5.3 Conclusions

Our findings in relation to our LIBT II pilot project confirm that Flipped Classrooms can improve students' learning experience. In general students enjoyed the flexibility offered by the video lectures and the extra in-class exercises, while

[102]The CUHK CTE questionnaire shows two scores, i.e. the raw score which counts all the responses and the adjusted score which excludes the lowest 10 % of the scores.

[103]The relatively low response rate in 2014/15 could be explained with the larger percentage of part-time students having registered for this session.

[104]*Supra*, 3.6.4.1.

not all of them used the video lectures for revision purpose. We sensed that students have a slight preference for face-to-face lectures over video lectures. The reason could be that students had developed a certain learning pattern relying on face-to face lectures during the initial nine sessions. Watching video lectures required students to make extra efforts to prepare for class in advance. Another explanation could be that despite all the efforts, video lectures are less engaging than face-to-face lecture.

Our findings seem to confirm the generally perceived advantages of Flipped Classrooms. Nevertheless, for a number of obvious reasons they cannot be regarded as the 'last word' on this topic. First, the LIBT II cohort was relatively small and we have only flipped two LIBT II sessions. The qualitative and quantitative information and data which we were able to develop do therefore by no means allow for a final assessment of the pedagogical viability of the Flipped Classroom model. In particular, we have not (yet) been able to generate reliable data on the question whether Flipped Classrooms do in fact lead to improved learning outcomes.[105] Another issue, which requires further attention, is the difference of the learning experience between full-time and part-time students on the one hand and between Chinese and non-Chinese students on the other hand.

Our pilot Flipped Classroom project has nevertheless allowed us to test many of the findings of our literature review. In particular, our pilot project has confirmed that it is in fact relatively easy to create Flipped Classrooms. And, the feedback from the LIBT II students will be valuable for designing courses with Flipped Classroom elements in the future.

[105] Compare *supra*, 6.5.1.3.

Chapter 7
Final Remarks

It was one of the main purposes of this study to conduct a comprehensive review of the literature on Flipped Classrooms so as to establish the basis for future research on this and related topics. We are confident that we have achieved this goal and hope that our study will encourage colleagues to experiment with this innovative teaching mode as well.

Our study shows that Flipped Classrooms are not the one and only solution for all pedagogical issues arising in the context of legal education. In fact, variety (of teaching modes) in itself seems to be key to success in law teaching. The use of Flipped Classrooms can be a very powerful tool in this regard. Our own case study has been a new, exciting and very meaningful experience to us which has tremendously enriched our understanding of law teaching pedagogy.

As pointed out several times, publicly available materials and data on Flipped Classrooms are still rare. It is consequently too early to pass final judgment on the viability of Flipped Classrooms. We believe that it would be very helpful for any future Flipped Classroom project (as well as other e-learning initiatives) to be accompanied by a structured research project. Related results should be published for the benefit of further innovation in the area of legal education.

Appendix A: List of Law School Websites Searched

List A.1 U.K. Law Schools

1. Anglia Ruskin University
2. Bournemouth University
3. Brunel University

The original version of this chapter was revised: The erratum to this chapter is available at 10.1007/978-981-10-0479-7_8

L.-C. Wolff and J. Chan, *Flipped Classrooms for Legal Education*,
SpringerBriefs in Law, DOI 10.1007/978-981-10-0479-7_7

4. Cardiff University
5. City Law School
6. City University London
7. Coventry University
8. Durham University
9. King's College London
10. Kingston University
11. Lancaster University
12. Leeds Metropolitan University
13. Liverpool John Moores University
14. London Metropolitan University
15. London School of Economics and Political Science
16. London South Bank University
17. Middlesex University
18. Newcastle University
19. Nottingham Trent University
20. Oxford Brookes University
21. Oxford Institute of Legal Practice
22. Queen's University of Belfast
23. Staffordshire University
24. Swansea University
25. University of Aberdeen
26. University of Bedfordshire
27. University of Birmingham
28. University of Brighton
29. University of Bristol
30. University of Cambridge
31. University of Central Lancashire
32. University College London
33. University of East Anglia
34. University of East London
35. University of Edinburgh
36. University of Essex
37. University of Exeter
38. University of Glasgow
39. University of Hull
40. University of Keele
41. University of Kent
42. University of Law
43. University of Leeds
44. University of Leicester
45. University of Lincoln
46. University of Liverpool
47. University of London
48. University of Manchester

49. University of Nottingham
50. University of Oxford
51. University of Reading
52. University of Sheffield
53. University of Southampton
54. University of Strathclyde
55. University of Surrey
56. University of Sussex
57. University of Teesside
58. University of Warwick
59. University of Wolverhampton

List A.2 U.S. Law Schools

1. American University
2. Arizona State University
3. Baylor University
4. Boston College
5. Boston University
6. Brigham Young University
7. Brooklyn Law School
8. Case Western Reserve University
9. Catholic University of America
10. Chapman University
11. College of William & Mary
12. Columbia University
13. Cornell University
14. DePaul University
15. Duke University
16. Emory University
17. Florida State University
18. Fordham University
19. George Mason University
20. George Washington University
21. Georgetown University
22. Georgia State University
23. Harvard University
24. Hofstra University
25. Illinois Institute of Technology
26. Indiana University
27. Indiana University, Bloomington
28. Lewis & Clark College
29. Louisiana State University
30. Loyola Marymount University
31. Loyola University Chicago

32. New York University
33. Northeastern University
34. Northwestern University
35. Ohio State University
36. Pennsylvania State University
37. Pepperdine University
38. Rutgers, State University of New Jersey, Camden
39. Rutgers, State University of New Jersey, Newark
40. Santa Clara University
41. Seattle University
42. Seton Hall University
43. Southern Methodist University
44. St. John's University
45. Stanford University
46. Syracuse University
47. Temple University
48. Tulane University
49. University of Alabama
50. University of Arizona
51. University of Arkansas
52. University of California, Berkley
53. University of California, Davis
54. University of California, Hastings College of the Law
55. University of California, Los Angeles
56. University of Chicago
57. University of Cincinnati
58. University of Colorado Boulder
59. University of Connecticut
60. University of Denver (Sturm)
61. University of Florida
62. University of Georgia
63. University of Hawaii
64. University of Houston
65. University of Illinois, Urbana
66. University of Iowa
67. University of Kansas
68. University of Kentucky
69. University of Maryland
70. University of Miami
71. University of Michigan
72. University of Minnesota, Twin Cities
73. University of Missouri
74. University of Nebraska

75. University of Nevada
76. University of New Mexico
77. University of North Carolina, Chapel Hill
78. University of Notre Dame
79. University of Oklahoma
80. University of Oregon
81. University of Pennsylvania Law School
82. University of Pittsburgh
83. University of Richmond
84. University of San Diego
85. University of San Francisco
86. University of Southern California Law School
87. University of Tennessee
88. University of Texas
89. University of the Pacific
90. University of Utah
91. University of Virginia
92. University of Washington
93. University of Wisconsin-Madison
94. Vanderbilt University Law School
95. Villanova University
96. Wake Forest University
97. Washington and Lee University
98. Washington University
99. West Virginia University
100. William Mitchell College of Law
101. Yale University
102. Yeshiva University

List A.3 Law Schools in Australia and New Zealand

1. Australian National University
2. Bond University
3. Charles Darwin University
4. Deakin University
5. Edith Cowan University
6. Flinders University
7. Griffith University
8. James Cook University
9. Macquarie University
10. Monash University
11. Murdoch University
12. Queensland University of Technology

13. RMIT University
14. Southern Cross University
15. University of Adelaide
16. University of Auckland
17. University of Canterbury (New Zealand)
18. University of Melbourne
19. University of New England
20. University of New South Wales
21. University of Newcastle
22. University of Notre Dame Australia
23. University of Otago
24. University of Queensland
25. University of Sydney
26. University of Tasmania
27. University of Technology Sydney
28. University of Waikato (New Zealand)
29. University of Western Australia
30. University of Western Sydney
31. University of Wollongong
32. Victoria University
33. Victoria University of Wellington

List A.4 Asian Law Schools

1. China University of Political Science and Law
2. City University of Hong Kong
3. Fudan University
4. Korea University
5. Kyushu University
6. Nanyang Technological University
7. National Taiwan University
8. National University of Singapore
9. Peking University
10. Renmin (People's) University of China
11. Seoul National University
12. Shanghai Jiao Tong University
13. Singapore Management University
14. The Chinese University of Hong Kong
15. Tsinghua University
16. University Malaya
17. University of Hong Kong
18. University of Tokyo
19. Yonsei University

Appendix B: Checklist—Developing Flipped Classrooms?

Step 1 Planning[1]

Step 1.1 Planning—to flip or not to flip?

- What is the educational purpose of the subject?[2]
- What student learning outcomes do you want to achieve?[3] What knowledge, skills or abilities will students acquire from the course?
- What activities will help students to achieve the learning goals?[4] If you believe that more in-class activity could help achieving the learning goals, then you may consider flipping.

Step 1.2 Planning—choose the right topics

- FLIP content that is:
  - 'straight forward concept(s), basic application(s), or demonstration of a skill'[5] or
  - 'confusing, yet can be previewed to assist class discussion'.[6]
- Suitable content includes:
  - 'preview and review of concepts'
  - theory or legal definitions,
  - summary of the law or previously discussed cases,
  - 'basic skills to be modeled or discussed',
  - basic problems and application of the law, and
  - 'feedback on assignments'.[7]
- DON'T FLIP content:
  - that is adequately covered by printed materials,[8]
  - where you expect student resistance or unpredictable questions,[9]

---

[1]Supra, 4.2.

[2]Deakin Learning Futures Teaching Development Team, p. 10.

[3]Hess, p. 79.

[4]*Ibid.*

[5]Upchurch, p. 4.

[6]*Ibid.*

[7]*Ibid*, pp. 4–5.

[8]*Ibid.*

[9]*Ibid.*

- that is difficult to be delivered in a 10–20-minute recording, or
- that is unsuitable to be presented 'in a visually engaging format'.[10]

- 'Start small'. It is NOT necessary to flip the entire course.[11]

Step 1.3 Planning—redesign your course

- Plan carefully which components are best delivered by the video/audio lectures and which are best reserved for in-class activities.[12]
- Teachers should:
  - optimize the in-class time to enrich students' learning experience rather than replacing in-class time with online modules,[13]
  - provide in-class interactive guidance on the topics covered by the videos.[14]
- Teachers should NOT use in-class time to teach students additional content.[15]
- Examples of in-class activities:
  - teacher-directed questions and answers,
  - individual work,
  - student-directed small group discussions,
  - presentations,
  - problem-solving simulations, and
  - brief-lectures.[16]
- Out-of-class content may also include assigned reading materials.[17] Teachers may request students to complete tasks while watching or after watching online videos to reinforce the learning experience.[18]

Step 1.4 Planning—designing the video/audio lectures

- How long should the video/audio lectures be? Try to make short lectures (between 10 and 20 min).[19] Smaller files are easier to edit, upload, access and digest.
- Is the additional amount of out-of-class work realistic? Students' overload must be avoided.[20]

---

[10]*Ibid.*

[11]*Ibid*, p. 5; Compare CADQ, pp. 2–3; Dewey, p. 2.

[12]Dewey, p. 3.

[13]Upchurch, p. 5.

[14]*Ibid.*

[15]*Ibid.*

[16]*Ibid*, Davis/Neary/Vaughn, p. 18.

[17]*Ibid*; Dewey, p. 4.

[18]Upchurch, p. 6.

[19]Compare Le Brun/Johnstone, p. 260; Ireland, p. 150.

[20]Dewey, p. 3; *supra*, 3.6.5.

Step 1.5 Planning—check technical readiness and resources

- Technical readiness
  - Do you or the IT department have the technical skills to produce Flipped Classrooms, i.e. do the recording, editing and uploading?
  - Do you have sufficient time?[21]
- Resources
  - Does your institution/do you have the necessary equipment or technology available?
  - Is there any studio or assigned site for recording?[22]
  - If you choose the 'screen capture approach', a desktop rather than a laptop computer may be more suitable.[23]
  - Does your institution have/do you have editing software which is compatible with the operating system?[24]
  - Do your students/does your institution have the necessary device(s) to access video/audio lectures?
  - Is additional investment necessary? Do you have access to the necessary funding sources?

Step 2 Production[25]

Step 2.1 Production—preparation

- Prepare a script before recording and practice.[26]
- Speak with precision and clearly during the recording.[27] Avoid unnecessary motion, irrelevant images or noises.[28]
- Remember to check lighting.[29]
- Make recordings in one take and avoid obsession with editing out the 'ums' and small errors.[30]
- Experiment with recording first to check the lighting, sound and quality of the recording before starting the production.

---

[21]Dewey, p. 2; Ireland, p. 155; Beck, p. 279; Davis/Neary/Vaughn, p. 18.

[22]Dewey, p. 3.

[23]Lihosit/Larrington, p. 10.

[24]*Ibid.*

[25]*Supra*, 4.31.

[26]Deakin Learning Futures Teaching Development Team, p. 14.

[27]The Blue Paper, p. 26.

[28]Upchurch, pp. 5–6.

[29]Deakin Learning Futures Teaching Development Team, p. 17.

[30]Upchurch, p. 5.

Step 2.2 Production—video or audio lecture?[31]

- Do you understand your students' learning preference?[32] Do they prefer video or audio lectures? Can you provide both to satisfy different learning needs?
- Do your students have the necessary device to view or listen to video/audio lectures?
- Are the video/audio formats chosen compatible with students' devices, operating systems and browsers?[33]

Step 2.3a Production—choosing the 'white board approach'[34]

- The teacher 'simply tapes himself or herself in front of a white board or flip chart'.[35]
- Resources:
  - equipment: a webcam, video camera or inbuilt camera on any mobile device. Use of external microphone may improve the audio quality.[36]
  - editing software: simple editing apps are usually inbuilt in the video camera or mobile device. If you need to edit the video on a computer, editing software such as Windows Movie Maker for PC or iMovie for Mac is necessary.[37]
- Teachers are advised to use the 'white board approach'
  - if teacher's presence is regarded important.[38]
  - for 'welcome messages, to introduce topics, provide overviews and address frequently asked questions'.[39]
  - unless the lecture concerns an often changing topics.
  - to consider providing students a written script to read while watching the video lectures.[40]

Step 2.3b Production—choosing the 'screen capture approach'[41]

- The 'screen capture approach' matches the teacher's voice with an online presentation normally providing explanations and examples around a PowerPoint slideshow.[42]

[31] *Supra*, 4.3.2–4.

[32] Gerdy et al., p. 266, *supra*, 4.3.5.

[33] Lihosit/Larrington, p. 10; *supra*, 4.5.

[34] *Supra*, 3.5.2 and 4.3.2.

[35] Upchurch, p. 3.

[36] Deakin Learning Futures Teaching Development Team, p. 17.

[37] *Ibid*, p. 20, Module 2, Table 6.

[38] *Supra*, 3.5.2.

[39] *Ibid*, p. 17.

[40] The Blue Paper, p. 27.

[41] *Supra*, 3.5.2 and 4.3.3.

[42] Deakin Learning Futures Teaching Development Team, p. 21.

- Resources:
  - equipment: a desktop computer.
  - editing software: Camstasia, Captivate, Echo 360 Personal Capture, Educreations, Jing, MediaSite, Screener, Screencast-O-Matic and Snagit.[43]
- Teachers are advised to use the 'screen capture approach':
  - if it is intended to satisfy visual and auditory learning needs of students.;
  - if they are confident with their technical skills.
  - if it is expected that certain parts of the lecture content will require future updating.

Step 2.3c Production—choosing the audio-only format[44]

- Only teacher's voice is recorded.
- Resources
  - equipment: a smartphone or tablet. Quality of sound should be at FM radio level for optimal listening.[45]
  - recording software: Recordium and Voice Recorder HD for iOS and Voice Pro and Voice Recorder Pro for Android.[46]
  - editing software: the mobile device usually comes with simple editing apps. For more sophisticated editing, use audio editing applications, such as Audacity for a PC or GarageBand for a Mac.[47]
- The audio-only format requires the lowest budget and technical skills.[48]
- Consider providing students materials to read while listening to the audio lectures.

Step 2.4 Alternative to production—OERs[49]

- If producing your own video/audio lecture is not an option, you may opt for OERs instead—be prepared, however, for the time and effort to locate and integrate 'foreign' materials into your own course.
- OERs are e.g. available at:
  - iTunes U
  - YouTube EDU
  - MERLOT
  - MIT OpenCourseWare

---

[43]*Ibid*, p. 21, Module 2, Table 7; Lihosit/Larrington, p. 10; Davis/Neary/Vaughn, p. 14.

[44]*Supra*, 3.5.3 and 4.3.4.

[45]Audacity, under Sample Rates.

[46]Deakin Learning Futures Teaching Development Team, p. 15, Module 2, Table 5.

[47]*Ibid*, p. 14.

[48]Martin, p. 76.

[49]*Supra*, 5.4.

Step 3 Distribution[50]

Step 3.1a Distribution—by existing institutional platforms

- Does your institution have existing platforms (Blackboard, WebCT, and TWEN) which allow uploading of digital files?[51]
- Is 'streaming' or similar technology available?[52] Check with the IT department whether your video/audio files are of the right size for uploading and downloading.[53]
- Does the platform have sufficient bandwidth to accommodate simultaneous access by students? If not, the limit on access numbers must be known in advance to allocate access time to students.[54]
- Does the server have enough storage for all the digital files or can an individual storage quota be allocated to the 'flipped' course?[55]
- Are there any institutional policies regarding the uploading and downloading of digital files in the university?

Step 3.1b Distribution—by private platforms[56]

- Examples of private platforms:
  - YouTube
  - podcasting
  - Vimeo
  - SoundCloud
- Since this type of open channel makes the files publicly accessible, the protection of digital files must be ensured possibly with the help of IT colleagues.[57]
- Available online storage services are:
  - Portfolio
  - OneDrive for Business
  - GoogleDrive
  - Cloudstor.[58]
- The use of private platforms may entail that the teacher himself/herself rather than the IT department has to be responsible for any technical follow-ups.

---

[50]*Supra*, 4.4.

[51]Deakin Learning Futures Teaching Development Team, p. 19, Module 2, Table 5.

[52]*Supra*, 4.4.

[53]*Ibid.*

[54]The Blue Paper, p. 15.

[55]*Ibid*, p. 20.

[56]*Supra*, 4.4.

[57]The Blue Paper, p. 27.

[58]Deakin Learning Futures Teaching Development Team, Module 2, Table 4, p. 13.

Step 4: Others

- In order to gain full cooperation from students, adequate communication is necessary in relation to purpose, benefits and implementation of Flipped Classroom concept.[59]
- Explain to students the structure of the course and the importance on viewing or listening to online lectures before coming to class.
- Offer technical training and support.

Appendix C: Materials Related to the Case Study

Table C.1 OER videos on LIBT II topics

Recommended sources for topic: due diligence		
No.	Videos	Length
1	Title: Legal Due Diligence Provider: Thomas Lloyd Group (Law firm) Link: https://www.youtube.com/watch?v=s-6fMku5zQI	9:58
2	Title: Due Diligence in China: Paper VS Reality—Michael D. Lee, Pamir Law Group Provider: iChinaForum.com Link: https://www.youtube.com/watch?v=kXkFTDVzqgc	9:25
3	Title: Bob Horstmeyer—GrowthPoint MD—Representations and Warranties Provider: Growth Point Partners Link: www.youtube.com/watch?v=LttDZtAWVuo	1:17
Suggested sources		
4	Title: Due Diligence, What is it and What to expect Provider: Pacific Business Brokers Inc. Link: https://www.youtube.com/watch?v=HZb6_IJMaUM	6:43
5	Title: Due Diligence During the M&A Process—Part 1 Provider: GeorgePShenas (Law firm) Link: https://www.youtube.com/watch?v=AKKvXhPiVdw	9:28
Recommended sources for topic: contract drafting		
1	Title: Case Downtown—'Best Practices for Clear Contract Drafting,' 5.9.12, Professor Carolyn Seymour Provider: The City Club of Cleveland Link: https://www.youtube.com/watch?v=GQRMNLh8yIo	1:00:43
2	Title: Contract Drafting in 90 min Provider: EmorySchoolofLaw Link: https://www.youtube.com/watch?v=d3VuHSmeAIw	1:33:37 (from 56:36–1:17:00)

(continued)

[59]*Supra*, 3.6.4.4.

Table C.1 (continued)

Videos explaining common law contract law		
1	Title: Contract Law—Introduction and Offer Part 1 Publisher: Law Sessions Link: http://www.youtube.com/watch?v=yGNvMxpK9rk	11:30
2	Title: Contract Law—Contents of a Contract Part 1 Publisher: Law Sessions Link: http://www.youtube.com/watch?v=MyF2k7Fs8B8	17:34
3	Title: How is a contract formed? Publisher: DevantLtd Link: http://www.youtube.com/watch?v=hsSzfDBo_f8	7:15
Recommended sources for topic: conflict of laws		
1	Title: Commercial Conflict of Laws Provider: University of Birmingham Link: https://www.youtube.com/watch?v=-d4RqJTaYP0&index=4&list=PL0vDVmcRRpvSDik__ExjMaWhK0ptzpjda	3:27 (from 0:00 to 3:00)
Recommended sources for topic: case study: Mainland China's Investment Law System (1) & (2)		
1	Title: Due Diligence in China: Paper VS Reality—Michael D. Lee, Pamir Law Group Provider: iChinaForum.com Link: https://www.youtube.com/watch?v=kXkFTDVzqgc	9:25
2	Title: M&A in 2014: Mergers and acquisitions in China Provider: Norton Rose Fulbright Link: https://www.youtube.com/watch?v=IhL3dTGNJoU	58:41

Table C.2 List of videos produced as (flipped) LIBT II online lectures

Week 10				
No.	Title	Content	Length	Size (MB)
1	IBT II 2014–15 Week 10 (1)	Introduction	36 m 24 s	131
2	IBT II 2014–15 Week 10 (2)	China's Private International Investment Law	17 m	56.3
3	IBT II 2014–15 Week 10 (3)	Government Control	13 m 20 s	41.1
4	IBT II 2014–15 Week 10 (4)	Structuring Investment Projects in China	29 m 39 s	87
Week 11				
5	IBT II 2014–15 Week 11 (1)	M&A in China	46 m 23 s	153.7
6	IBT II 2014–15 Week 11 (2)	Chinese Outbound Investments	9 m 14 s	30.5
7	IBT II 2014–15 Week 11 (3)	Merger Control & National Security Review	14 m 18 s	49.8

(continued)

Table C.2 (continued)

Week 10				
No.	Title	Content	Length	Size (MB)
8	IBT II 2014–15 Week 11 (4)	Labour Issues	9 m 2 s	30
Suggested viewing				
No.	Content	Length		
9	Title: 35 Years of Chinese Investment Law—Facts, Trends, Stories Link: http://www.cpr.cuhk.edu.hk/cutv/detail/562	53 m 50 s From 11 m 17 s ff		

Table C.3 LIBT II reading suggestions

Week 10	
Topics	Reading suggestions
• Introduction • China's Private International Investment Law • Government Control • Structuring Investment Projects in China	• Wolff, Mergers & Acquisitions in China, 4th ed. (Hong Kong 2010), pp. 1–74 • Wolff, PRC Company Law: 'One Country, Many Systems?', Hong Kong Lawyer 3/2001, pp. 37–42 • Wolff, Pathological Foreign Investment Projects in China: Patchwork or Trendsetting of the Supreme People's Court?, The International Lawyer (Fall 2010) Volume 44 No. 3, pp. 1001–1018
Week 11	
• M&A in China • Chinese Outbound Investments • Merger Control & • National Security Review • Labour Issues	• Wolff, Mergers & Acquisitions in China, 4th ed. (Hong Kong 2010), pp. 75–115, pp. 145–179, pp. 195–212 • Wolff, Chinese Outbound Investments in the Food Sector: Hungry for Much More!, Food and Drug Law Journal Vol. 69 No. 3 (2014), pp. 399–428

Table C.4 Questionnaire (raw form)
Part I—please pick one

	Answer
I am: A. Full-time student B. Part-time student	
I am from: A. Hong Kong B. Mainland China C. Macao or Taiwan D. Asian Countries/Regions other than A, B or C E. Countries/Regions other than A, B, C or D	

(continued)

Table C.4 (continued)

	Answer
I have watched one or more of the video lectures: A. 0 times B. 1–5 times C. 6–10 times D. more than 10 times **If your answer is A, go to Part II, IV (a) and (b) and V.** **If your answer is B, C or D, go to Part III (a)–(c), IV (a) and (b) and V**	

Part II—Please answer this part if you have NOT watched the video lectures at all. Use numbers (1–5) to indicate your agreement with the below statements:

1 = strongly disagree
2 = disagree
3 = neutral
4 = agree
5 = strongly agree.

	Answer
1. I did not know that video lectures were available.	
2. I did not know the importance of watching video lectures.	
3. I had a device but did not know how to watch or download the video lectures.	
4. I had a device but could not find time to download or watch the video lectures.	
5. I do not like watching video lectures. I prefer face-to-face lectures instead.	
6. I do not like lectures at all. I prefer reading the relevant materials instead.	
7. I will watch the video lectures at least once before the exam.	

Part III (a)—Please answer this part if you have watched AT LEAST ONE of the video lectures. Use numbers (1–5) to indicate your agreement with the below statements:

1 = strongly disagree
2 = disagree
3 = neutral
4 = agree
5 = strongly agree.

	Answer
1. The visual quality of the video lectures was clear.	
2. The audio quality of the video lectures was clear.	
3. The speaker's presentation was clear.	
4. The content was delivered at an appropriate speed.	
5. I did not experience difficulties in downloading.	
6. The video lectures were of the right length (not too long, not short).	
7. If I were given a choice, I would choose face-to-face lectures instead of watching video lectures.	
8. If I were given a choice, I would choose watching video lectures instead of face-to-face lectures.	
9. I will watch all or some of the video lectures again before the exam.	
10. I like video lectures because they allow more time for in-class exercises.	
11. The video lectures help me understand the topics.	
12. The video lectures help revision.	
13. The video lectures give me flexibility when preparing for in-class sessions.	
14. The video lectures allow me to skip classes.	
15. I do not like face-to-face lectures.	
16. It is difficult to use the video lectures.	
17. It is time-consuming to watch all the video lectures.	

Part III (b)—Please answer this part if you have watched AT LEAST ONE of the video lectures

<table>
<tr><td rowspan="2">1. I watched one or more video lecture(s)…
(Tick (√) one or more boxes.)</td><td colspan="3">before class</td><td colspan="2">after class</td></tr>
<tr><td colspan="3"></td><td colspan="2"></td></tr>
<tr><td rowspan="2">2. I watched video lecture(s) when I was …
(Tick (√) one or more boxes.)</td><td>at home</td><td>at school</td><td>travelling</td><td>exerci-sing</td><td>elsewhere</td></tr>
<tr><td></td><td></td><td></td><td></td><td></td></tr>
<tr><td>3. The video lecture(s) I liked best were: …
(Write down the no. or the topic of the video lecture(s).)</td><td colspan="5"></td></tr>
</table>

Part III (c)—Please answer this part if you have watched AT LEAST ONE of the video lectures. Use numbers (1–5) to indicate your agreement with the below statements:

1 = strongly disagree
2 = disagree
3 = neutral
4 = agree
5 = strongly agree.

	Answer
1. I could understand the lecture topics by reading relevant materials alone (without watching the video lectures).	
2. I enjoyed the in-class exercises in week 10 and 11 more than the exercises in other sessions.	
3. I have participated more actively in in-class exercises in week 10 and 11 than the other sessions.	
4. I prefer to have more time for in-class exercises rather than spending in-class time listening to lectures.	
6. I look forward to taking courses using video lectures in the future.	

Part IV (a)—For students who have experienced TECHNICAL PROBLEMS

1. The technical problem concerned… (Tick (√) one or more boxes.)	Downloading	Device not compatible	Problems locating the videos	Others

Part IV (b)—For students who have experienced TECHNICAL PROBLEMS. Use numbers (1–5) to indicate your agreement with the below statements:

1 = strongly disagree
2 = disagree
3 = neutral
4 = agree
5 = strongly agree.

	Answer
1. The university technical support team was friendly	
2. The technical problem was solved after seeking assistance from the technical support team	
3. I have sought help from people other than the technical support team	

Part V: Additional Comments—if any—on the LIBT II video lectures.

Table C.5 Data gathered via the questionnaire
Total number of students participating: 125

Part I	No of students	%
Number of Full-time students:	102	81.6
Number of Part-time students:	23	18.4

Number of students from:		
Hong Kong	31	24.8
Mainland China	87	69.6
Asian Countries other than Hong Kong, Mainland China, Macao or Taiwan	2	1.6
Countries other than above	5	4.0

Part I		
Number of students who have watched at least one of the video lectures:	121	96.8
Number of students who have not watched any video lectures	4	3.2

Part II—questions related to non-watchers					
Part III (a)					%
	S. disagree	Disagree	Neutral	Agree	S. agree
1. The visual quality of the video lectures was clear.	0.0	3.2	12.0	40.8	40.8
2. The audio quality of the video lectures was clear.	0.0	3.2	5.6	38.4	49.6
3. The speaker's presentation was clear.	0.0	3.2	5.6	44.0	44.0
4. The content was delivered at an appropriate speed.	0.0	1.6	10.4	48.0	36.8
5. I did not experience difficulties in downloading.	11.2	14.4	14.4	20.8	36.0
6. The video lectures were of the right length (not too long not short).	0.8	6.4	12.8	40.0	36.8
7. If I were given a choice, I would choose face-to-face lectures instead of watching video lectures.	3.2	10.4	28.8	19.2	35.2
8. If I were given a choice, I would choose watching video lectures instead of face-to-face lectures.	25.6	30.4	28.0	7.2	5.6
9. I will watch all or some of the video lectures again before the exam.	4.8	18.4	25.6	34.4	13.6
10. I like video lectures because they allow more time for in-class exercises.	2.4	12.0	32.0	32.0	18.4
11. The video lectures help me understand the topics.	0.0	3.2	16.0	46.4	31.2

(continued)

Table C.5 (continued)

Part III (a)					%
12. The video lectures help revision.	0.8	3.2	27.2	42.4	23.2
13. The video lectures give me flexibility when preparing for in-class sessions.	1.6	2.4	20.0	42.4	30.4
14. The video lectures allow me to skip classes.	42.4	32.8	15.2	4.8	1.6
15. I do not like face-to-face lectures.	57.6	32.8	4.8	0.0	1.6
16. It is difficult to use the video lectures.	42.4	31.2	13.6	7.2	2.4
17. It is time-consuming to watch all the video lectures.	23.2	32.0	21.6	12.0	8.0

Part III (b)						%
1. I watched the video lectures…	Before class	After class	Both	Others	No reply	
	80.0	5.6	8.8	0.8	1.6	
2. I watched video lecture(s) when I was…	At home	At school	Travelling	Elsewhere	At home and at school	At home/travelling or others
	67.2	11.2	0.0	1.6	8.8	6.4
3. The video lecture(s) I liked best were:…	40 students like week 10; 23 students like week 11; 7 students like all. One likes the public lecture					

Part III (c)					
	S. disagree	Disagree	Neutral	Agree	S. agree
1. I could understand the lecture topics by reading relevant materials alone (without watching the video lectures).	3.2	29.6	28.8	28.0	6.4
2. I enjoyed the in-class exercises in week 10 and 11 more than the exercises in other sessions.	3.2	8.0	33.6	34.4	16.8
3. I have participated more actively in in-class exercises in week 10 and 11 than the other sessions.	2.4	4.0	19.2	48.0	21.6
4. I prefer to have more time for in-class exercises rather than spending in-class time listening to lectures.	4.0	14.4	36.0	26.4	13.6
5. I look forward to taking courses using video lectures in the future.	10.4	16.0	33.6	25.6	8.8

Part IV (a)					%
	Down-loading	Device not compatible	Problems locating the videos	Others	No problem
The technical problem concerned…	24.8	11.2	2.4	6.4	52.0

(continued)

Table C.5 (continued)

Part IV (b)					%
	S. disagree	Disagree	Neutral	Agree	S. agree
1. The university technical support team was friendly.	0.0	3.2	4.8	7.2	2.4
2. The technical problem was solved after seeking assistance from the technical support team.	0.8	2.4	6.4	4.8	1.6
3. I have sought help from people other than the technical support team.	0.8	3.2	0.8	8.8	1.6

Table C.6 Echo 360 data re visits of (flipped) LIBT II online lectures

Week 10 videos			
Data were collected prior to the LIBT II morning class of 16 March at 9 am and prior to the LIBT II evening class of 16 March at 6 pm. To assess if additional students have viewed the online lectures prior to the LIBT II examination, data were again collected on 23 April, i.e. one day after the LIBT II examination. The numbers of viewers are therefore set out below for each category as follows: 16 March 9 am/16 March 6 pm/23 April			
Video	Unique views	Cumulative views	Average completion
10 (1)	91/94/100	173/185/217	85/85/85
10 (2)	70/81/86	106/124/144	92/93/94
10 (3)	69/81/87	106/124/126	90/91/92
10 (4)	62/73/83	98/119/150	87/92/92
Week 11 videos			
Data were collected prior to the LIBT II morning class of 23 March at 9 am and prior to the LIBT II evening class of 23 March at 6 pm. To assess if additional students have viewed the online lectures prior to the LIBT II examination, data were again collected on 23 April, i.e. one day after the LIBT II examination. The numbers of viewers are therefore set out for each category as follows: 23 March 9 am/23 March 6 pm/23 April			
Video	Unique views	Cumulative views	Average completion
11 (1)	74/86/96	167/204/258	86/86/88
11 (2)	63/76/87	81/96/115	90/91/90
11 (3)	61/76/82	82/100/116	88/88/88
11 (4)	56/67/77	66/81/98	89/88/88

Erratum to: Flipped Classrooms for Legal Education

Erratum to:
Chapter 7 in: L.-C. Wolff and J. Chan
***Flipped Classrooms for Legal Education*,**
SpringerBriefs in Law, DOI 10.1007/978-981-10-0479-7_7

The appendices A, B and C should be replaced from the book's back matter to the "final remarks" section at the end of Chap. 7.

The references should be left as is at the book's back matter itself.

The updated original online version for this book can be found at 10.1007/978-981-10-0479-7_7

L.-C. Wolff and J. Chan, *Flipped Classrooms for Legal Education*,
SpringerBriefs in Law, DOI 10.1007/978-981-10-0479-7_8

References

Note: All online sources were last visited on 25 August 2015 unless otherwise indicated below.

Articles/Theses/Papers

Abrams, Jamie R., Reframing the Socratic Method. 64 *Journal of Legal Education* (2014 2015) pp. 562-585.

Adams, Andrew et al., Use of open educational resources in higher education. 44 *British Journal of Educational Technology* (2014) pp. 149-150.

Appleby, Gabrielle et al., Critical Thinking in Legal Education: Our Journey. 23 (345) *Legal Education Review* (2013) pp. 345-377.

Asarta, Carlos. J. & Schimdt, James.R., The Choice of Reduced Seat Time in a Blended Course. 27 *Internet and Higher Education* (2015) pp. 24-31.

Battaglino, Tamara et al., 'The Costs of Online Learning' in *A Working Paper Series from the Thomas B. Fordham Institute* (2012). http://edex.s3-us-west-2.amazonaws.com/publication/pdfs/20120110-the-costs-of-online-learning_7.pdf.

Beck, Robert J., Teaching International Law as a Partially Online Course: The Hybrid/ Blended Approach to Pedagogy. 11 *International Studies. Perspectives* (2010) pp. 273-290.

Benjamin, Andres H et al., *The Role of Legal Education in Producing Psychological Distress Among Law Students and Lawyers*. 225 B. Found. Res. J. (1986) pp. 246-247.

Berger, Mitchell, Why the U.S. News and World Report Law School Rankings Are Both Useful and Important. 51 *Journal of Legal Education* (2001) pp. 487-502.

Binford, W. Warren H., New Ideas in Law and Legal Education: Envisioning a Twenty-First Century Legal Education. 43 *Washington University Journal of Law and Policy* (2013) pp. 157-186.

Blasi, Gary, What Lawyers Know: Lawyering Expertise, Cognitive Science, and the Functions of Theory. 45 *Journal of Legal Education* (September 1995) pp. 313-397.

Bloxham, Sefton Widening access and the use of ICT in legal education. 39 *The Law Teacher* (2005) pp. 93-105.

Boghossian, Peter, Socratic Pedagogy, Race, and Power: From People to Propositions, 10 *Education Policy Analysis Archives* (2002) pp. 1-9.

Boghossian, Peter, Socratic Pedagogy: Perplexity, Humiliation, Shame and a Broken Egg. 44 *Educational Philosophy and Theory* (2012) pp. 710-720.

The original version of the book backmatter was revised: Appendices have been moved to Chapter 7. The Erratum to the book backmatter is available at 10.1007/978-981-10-0479-7_8

L.-C. Wolff and J. Chan, *Flipped Classrooms for Legal Education*,
SpringerBriefs in Law, DOI 10.1007/978-981-10-0479-7

Bone, Alison, The twenty-first century law student. 43 *The Law Teacher* (2009) pp. 222-245.
Bos, Nynke et al., The use of recorded lectures in education and the impact on lecture attendance and exam performance. *British Journal of Educational Technology* (2015) pp. 1-12.
Boyle, Robin A. & Dunn, Rita, Teaching law students through individual learning styles. 62 *Albany Law Review* (1998) pp. 213-255.
Brittain, Sarah et al., Podcasting Lectures. 3 *Educause Quarterly* (2006) pp. 24-31.
Broadbent, Graeme & Sellman, Pamela Great expectation? Law schools, websites and "the student experience". 47 *The Law Teacher* (2013) pp. 44-63.
CADQ -Centre for Academic Development and Quality (CADQ), Nottingham Trent University, *CADQ Guide - The Flipped classroom.* (June 2013). www.ntu.ac.uk/adq.
Caron, Paul L. & Gely, Rafael, Taking Back the Law School Classroom: Using Technology to Foster Active Student Learning. 54 *Journal of Legal Education* (2004) pp. 551-569.
Carrington, Paul D., The Pedagogy of the Old Case Method: A Tribute to 'Bull' Warren. 59 *Journal of Legal Education* (2009) pp. 457-466.
Catley, Paul, One Lecturer's Experience of Blending E-learning with Traditional Teaching. 1 (2) *Brookes eJournal of Learning and Teaching* (Jan 2005). http://bejlt.brookes.ac.uk/paper/one-lecturers-experience-of-blending-e-learning-with-traditional-teaching/.
Chickering, Arthur W. & Gamson, Zelda F., Seven Principles for Good Practice in Undergraduate Education. *Washington Center News* (1987). http://wwwtemp.lonestar.edu/multimedia/SevenPrinciples.pdf.
Cohen, Anat & Nachmias, Rafi, A quantitative cost effectiveness model for Web-supported academic instruction. 9 *Internet and Higher Education* (2006) pp. 81-90.
Cohen, Anat & Nachmias, Rafi, Implementing a cost effectiveness analyzer for Web-supported academic instruction: a campus wide analysis. 2 *European Journal of Open, Distance and E-learning* (2009) pp. 1-8.
Dahlstrom, Eden, *ECAR Study Undergraduate Students and Information Technology 2012 (Research Paper)*, Educause Center For Applied Research (September 2012). http://www.educause.edu.ecar.
Davis, Laurel E et al., Teaching Advanced Legal Research in a Flipped Classroom. 22 *Perspectives: Teaching Legal Research and Writing* (2013) pp. 13-19.
Deakin Learning Futures Teaching Development Team, *Using audio and video for educational purposes: Modules 1-4* (2014). http://www.deakin.edu.au/__data/assets/pdf_file/0003/179013/Modules_1-4_Using_audio_and_video_for_educational_purposes-2014-02-28.pdf.
Dewey, Michelle Hook, The Upside-Down Classroom: How the flipped lecture model can be used in legal education. *Carolinas Legal Research and Writing Colloquium* (May 2013). http://lawteaching.org/conferences/2013/handouts/1c-Upside-DownClassroom.pdf.
Dey, Eric L. et al., Bringing the Classroom to the Web: Effects of Using New Technologies to Capture and Deliver Lectures. 50 *Research in Higher Education* (2009) pp. 377-393.
Diekema, Anne R. et al., Re-framing Information Literacy: Problem-Based Learning as Informed Learning. 33 *Library and Information Science Research* (2011), pp. 261-268.
Donahoe, Diana R., An Autobiography of a Digital Idea: From Waging War against Laptops to Engaging Students with Laptops. 54 *Journal of Legal Education* (2009) pp. 485-514.
Dunham, Catherine & Friedland, Steven I., Portable Learning for the 21st Century Law School: Designing a New Pedagogy for the Modern Global Context. 26 *The John Marshall Journal of Computer and Information Law* (2009) pp. 371-393.
Dziuban, Charles & Moskal, Patsy, A Course is a Course is a Course: Factor Invariance in Student Evaluation of Online, Blended, and Face-to-face Learning Environments. 14 *Internet and Higher Education* (2011) pp. 236-241.
Educause I- Educause Learning Initiative, *7 Things You should Know about Flipped Classrooms.* (2012). http://net.educause.edu/ir/library/pdf/eli7081.pdf.

Field, Sarah & Jones, Lucy, Innovations in Assessment: An investigation into the role of blended learning as a support mechanism for assessment. 44 (3) *The Law Teacher* (2010) pp. 378-390.
Fitzgerald Maureen F., Rite of Passage: The impact of teaching methods on first year law students. 42 *The Law Teacher* (2008) pp. 60-84.
Frank, Jerome, Why not a Clinical Lawyer School?. 8 *University of Pennsylvania Law Review* (1993) pp. 907-923.
Freeland, Steven et al., Crossing the Language and Cultural Divide – The Challenges of Educating Asian Law Students in a Globalising World. 14 *Legal Education Review* (2003) pp. 219-238.
Friedman, Peggy and Alley, Robert, Learning/Teaching Styles: Applying the Principles. 23 *Theory into Practice* (2003) pp. 77-81.
Friel, Terri et al., Using pedagogical dialogue as a vehicle to encourage faculty technology use. 53 *Computers & Education* (2009) pp. 300-307.
Galves, Fred, Will Video Kill the Radio Star? Visual Learning and the Use of Display Technology in the Law School Classroom. *University of Illinois Journal of Law, Technology & Policy* (2004) pp. 195-251.
Garlikov, R., *Having Understanding Versus Knowing Correct Explanations* (2000). http://www.garlikov.com/Interpretation.html.
Garner, David, Socratic Misogyny? – Analyzing Feminist Criticisms of Socratic Teaching in Legal Education. *Brigham Young University Law Review* (2000) pp. 1597-1650.
Gerdy, Kristin B. et al., Expanding Our Classroom Walls: Enhancing Teaching and learning through Technology. 11 *Journal of the Legal Writing Institute* (2005) pp. 263-294.
Giannakos, Michail et al., Exploring the relationship between video lecture usage patterns and students' attitudes. *British Journal of Educational Technology* (2015).
Ginns, Paul & Ellis, Robert, Quality in blended learning: Exploring the relationships between on-line and face-to-face teaching and learning. 10 *Internet and Higher Education* (2007) pp. 53–64.
Gottfredson, Nisha C., Identifying Predictors of Law Student Life Satisfaction. 58 *Journal of Legal Education* (2008) pp. 520-530.
Graham, Charles R. et al., A framework for institutional adoption and implementation of blended learning in higher education. 18 *Internet and Higher Education* (2013) pp. 4-14.
Hamdan, Noora et al., Flipped Learning Network, *The Flipped Learning Model: A White Paper based on the Literature Review titled a review of Flipped Learning.* (2013). http://www.flippedlearning.org/Page/64.
Harris, Debra & Susman, Susan D., Toward a More Perfect Union: Using Lawyering Pedagogy to Enhance Legal Writing Courses. 49 *Journal of Legal Education* (1999) pp. 185-202.
Harris, Phil & Beinart, Sarah, A Survey of law schools in the United Kingdom (2004). 39 *The Law Teacher* (2005) pp. 299-366.
Hasche, Annette, Teaching Writing in Law: A Model to Improve Student Learning. 3 *Legal Education Review* (1992) pp. 267-294.
Henriss-Anderssen, Diana, Using Interactive Teaching Strategies in Large Lectures: Some Personal Reflections. 14 *Legal Education Review* (2003-2004) pp. 181-201.
Henderson, William D., A Blueprint for Change. 40 *Pepperdine Law Review* (2012) pp. 461-508.
Hess, Gerald F., Symposium: The State and Future of Legal Education: Blended Courses in Law School: The Best of Online and Face-to-Face Learning?. 45 *McGeorge Law Review* (2013) pp. 51-84.
Hewitt, Anne, Can you learn to lawyer online? A blended learning environment case study. 49 (1) *The Law Teacher* (2015) pp. 92-121.
Hrastinski, Stefan, Asynchronous & Synchronous E-learning. 4 Educause Quarterly (2008). https://net.educause.edu/ir/library/pdf/eqm0848.pdf.
Illig, Robert C., The Oregon Method: An Alternative Model for Teaching Transactional Law. 59 *Journal of Legal Education* (2009) pp. 221-239.

Ireland, Jennifer, Blended Learning in Intellectual Property: The Best of Both Worlds. 18 *Legal Education Review* (2008) pp. 139-161.

Jones, Ida M., Can You See Me Now? Defining Teaching Presence in the Online Classroom Through Building a Learning Community. 28 *Journal of Legal Studies Education* (Winter/Spring 2011) pp. 67–116.

Kaminskaya, Elvira, International Research and Exchanges Board, University Administration Support Program, University of Central Florida *Teaching with Technology: A Case Study of Online Faculty Development at the University of Central Florida* (2006), www.irex.org/system/files/kaminskaya.pdf.

Kazlauska, Alanah & Robinson, Kathy, Podcasts are not for everyone. 43 (2) *British Journal of Educational Technology* (2012) pp. 321-330.

Kerr, Orin S., The Decline of the Socratic Method at Harvard. 78 *Nebraska Law Review* (1999) pp. 113-134.

Kift, Sally, Lawyering Skills: Finding their Place in Legal Education. 8 *Legal Education Review* (1997) pp. 43-73.

Korn, Jane, Teaching Talking: Oral Communication Skills in a Law course. 54 *Journal of Legal Education* (2004) pp. 588-596.

Lambert, Sarah & Brewer, Chris, 1st, 2nd and 3rd Generation Implementations of an eLearning Design: Re-Use from Postgraduate Law to Block/Online Engineering Course. 2 *Journal of Learning Design* (2007) pp. 70-82.

Lane, Andy & McAndrew, Patrick, Are open educational resources systematic or systemic change agents for teaching practice?. 41 *British Journal of Educational Technology* (2010) pp. 952-962.

Larcombe, Wendy et al., Performance in Law School: What Matters in the Beginning?. 18 *Legal Education Review* (2008) pp. 95-122.

Laster, Kathy, *Educating Cultured Lawyers*. Thesis (J.S.D.), Columbia University. (2002).

Lemmer, Catherine, A View from the Flip Side: Using the "Inverted Classroom" to enhance the Legal Information Literacy of the International LLM Student. 105 *Law Library Journal* (2013) pp. 461-491.

Leslie, Douglas L., How Not To Teach Contracts, and Any Other Course: PowerPoint, Laptops and the CaseFile Method. *44 Saint Louis University Law Journal* (2000), pp. 1289-1316.

Lihosit, Judith & Larrington, Jane, Flipping the Legal Research Classroom. 22 *Perspectives Teaching Legal Research and Writing* (2013) pp. 1-12.

Lonn, Steven & Teasley, Stephanie D., Podcasting in higher education: What are the implications for teaching and learning?. 12 *Internet and Higher Education* (2009) pp. 88-92.

López-Pérez, M. Victoria et al., Blended learning in higher education: Students' perceptions and their relation to outcomes. 56 *Computers and Education* (2011) pp. 818–826.

Lustbader, Paula, Teach in Context: Responding to Diverse Student Voices Helps All Students Learn. 48 *Journal of Legal Education* (1998) pp. 402-416.

Maharg, Paul, On the edge: ICT and the transformation of professional legal education. 3 *Web Journal of Current Legal Issues* (2006).

Martin, Peter W., Cornell's experience running online, inter-school law courses-an FAQ. 39 *The Law Teacher* (2005) pp. 70-81.

Matthew, Anne, Managing Distraction and Attention in Diverse Cohorts: 21st Century Challenges to Law Student Engagement. 12 *QUT Law and Justice Journal* (2012) pp. 45-65.

McCormack, Timothy LH & Simpson, Gerry J, Simulating Multilateral Treaty Making in the Teaching of International Law. 10 *Legal Education Review* (1999) pp. 61-82.

McKellar, Patricia & Maharg, Paul, Virtual learning environments: The alternative to the box under the bed. 39 *The Law Teacher* (2005) pp. 43-56.

Means, Barbara et al., Centre for Technology in Learning, U.S. Department of Education, *Evaluation of Evidence-Based Practices in Online Learning: A Meta-Analysis and Review of Online Learning Studies.* (September 2010). www2.ed.gov/rschstat/eval/tech/evidence-based-practices/finalreport.doc.

Micolich, Adam, The latent potential of YouTube – Will it become the 21st Century Lecturer's Film Archive?. CAL-laborate (2008) pp. 1-8. http://arxiv.org/ftp/arxiv/papers/0808/0808.3441.pdf.

Morris-Babb, Meredith & Henderson, Susie, An Experiment in Open-Access Textbook Publishing: Changing the World One Textbook at a Time. 43 *Journal of Scholarly Publishing* (2012) pp. 148-155.

Moskal, Patsy et al., Blended Learning: A Dangerous Idea?. 18 *Internet and Higher Education* (2013) pp. 15–23.

Nehme, Marina, Elearning and Students' Motivation. 20 *Legal Education Review* (2010) pp. 223-239.

Newman, Marie Stefanini, Not the Evil TWEN: How Online Course Management Software Supports Non-Linear Learning in Law Schools. 5 *Journal of High Technology Law* (2005) pp. 183-233.

Oblinger, Diana, What it means to education. 3 *Emerging technologies for learning* (2008) pp. 11-29.

Ocak, Mehmet Akif, Why are faculty members not teaching blended courses? Insights from faculty members. 56 *Computers & Education* (2011) pp. 689-699.

O'Donnell, Anthony, Thinking 'Culture' in Legal Education. 7 *Legal Education Review* (1996) pp. 135-154.

Owston, Ron et al., Lecture capture in large undergraduate classes: Student perceptions and academic performance. 14 *Internet and Higher Education* (2011) pp. 262-268.

Owston, Ron et al., Student perceptions and achievement in a university blended learning strategic initiative. 18 *Internet and Higher Education* (2013) pp. 38-46.

Paechter, Manuela & Maier, Brigitte, Online or face-to-face? Students' experiences and preferences in e-learning. 12 *Internet and Higher Education* (2010) pp. 292-297.

Pettys, Todd E., The Analytic Classroom. 60 *Buffalo Law Review* (2012) pp. 1255-1322.

Polding, Liz, Delivering Blended Legal Learning by Open Source Methods. *Journal of Information, Law and Technology* (January 2007) pp. 1-11.

Prensky, Marc, Digital Natives, Digital Immigrant Part 1. 9 (2) *On the Horizon* (2001) pp. 1-6.

Redmond, Paul & Roper, Christopher, the Steering Committee on the Review of Legal Education and Training in Hong Kong. *Legal Education and Training in Hong Kong Preliminary Review: Summary of Consultation Paper* (2000). http://www.hklawsoc.org.hk.

Roach, Cathaleen, A River Runs through it. Tapping into the Informational Stream to move Students from Isolation to Autonomy. 36 *Arizona Law Review* (1994) pp. 667-699.

Rochette, Annie, *Teaching and Learning in Canadian Legal Education: An empirical exploration.* These (D.C.L.), McGill University (Canada) (2011).

Ryan, Erin et al., When Socrates meet Confucius: Teaching Creative and Critical Thinking Across Cultures Through Multilevel Socratic Method. 92 *Nebraska Law Review* (2013-2014) pp. 289-348.

Saliba, Gina et al., Blended Learning Team, Learning and Teaching Unit, University of Western Sydney *Fundamental of Blended Learning* (2013). http://www.uws.edu.au/__data/assets/pdf_file/0004/467095/Fundamentals_of_Blended_Learning.pdf.

Schneider, Jack, Socrates and the madness of method. 94 *Phi Delta Kappan* (2012) pp. 26-29.

Schwartz, Michael Hunter, Teaching Law by Design: How Learning Theory and Instructional Design Can Inform and Reform Law Teaching. 38 *San Diego Law Review* (2001) pp. 347-462.

Sharpe, Rhona et al., The Higher Education Academy, *The undergraduate experience of blended e-learning: a review of UK literature and practice* (October 2006). https://www.heacademy.ac.uk/resources/detail/teachingandresearch/Undergraduate_Experience.

Slomanson, William R, Blended Classroom: A Flipped Classroom Experiment at the Lectern. 64 *Journal of Legal Education* (2014-2015) pp. 93-102.

Smith, Craig T., Technology and Legal Education: Negotiating the Shoals of Technocentrism, Technophobia, and Indifference. 1 *Journal of the Association of Legal Writing Directors* (2002) pp. 247-256.

Snowden, Kelly E., *Teacher perceptions of the flipped classroom: Using video lectures online to replace traditional in-class lectures.* Thesis (MA), University of North Texas (2012).

Stevens, Elizabeth et al., Equity, Diversity and Student Engagement in a Law School – A Case Study Approach. 16 *Legal Education Review* (2006) pp. 1-33.

Stropus, Ruta K, Mend it, Bend it and Extend it: The Fate of Traditional Law School Methodology in the 21st Century. 27 *Loyola University of Chicago Law Journal* (1996) pp. 449-489.

Sutton, Susan R., The Preservice Technology Training Experiences of Novice Teachers. 28 *Journal of Digital Learning in Teacher Education* (2011) pp. 39-47.

Taylor Janet A. & Newton, Diane, Beyond blended learning: A case study of institutional change at an Australian regional university. 18 *Internet and Higher Education* (2013) pp. 54-60.

Teich, Paul F., Research on American Law Teaching – Is There a Case Against the Case System?. 36 *Journal of Legal Education* (1986), pp. 167-188.

The Blue Paper - Working Group for Distance Learning in Legal Education, Harvard Law School, *Distance Learning in Legal Education: A Summary of Delivery Models, Regulatory Issues, and Recommended Practices* (2012). http://www2.stetson.edu/atc/wp-content/uploads/2013/11/Distance_Learning_in_Legal_Ed.pdf.

The Carnegie Report Summary - Sullivan, William M., The Carnegie Foundation for the Advancement of Teaching, Educating Lawyers – Summary. San Francisco: Jossey-Bass/Wiley (2007).

The Dearing Report - The National Committee of Inquiry into Higher Education, Her Majesty Stationery Office, *The Dearing Report Higher Education in the learning society.* (1997). http://www.educationengland.org.uk/documents/dearing1997/dearing1997.html.

Tomei, Lawrence A., The Impact of Online Teaching on Faculty Load: Computing the Ideal Class Size for Online Courses. 14 *Journal of Technology and Teacher Education* (2006) pp. 531-541.

Traphagan, T. et al., Impact of class lecture webcasting on attendance and learning. 58 (1) *Educational Technology Research & Development* (2010) pp. 19–37.

Tweed, Roger G & Lehman, Darrin R., Learning Considered Within a Cultural Context: Confucian and Socratic Approaches. 57 *American Psychologist* (2002) pp. 89-99.

Tyler Melissa Conley & Cukier, Naomi, Nine Lessons for Teaching Negotiation Skills. 15 *Legal Education Review* (2005) pp. 61-86.

Upchurch, Angela, Optimizing the Law School Classroom through the 'Flipped' Classroom Model. *The Law Teacher* (Fall 2013).

Wallace, Albin, Social Learning Platforms and the Flipped Classroom. 4 *International Journal of Information and Education Technology* (August 2014) pp. 293-296.

Wenk, Bruno, Open educational resources (OER) inspire teaching and learning. (April 2010) *Education Engineering* pp. 435-442.

Wilcox, Jamison, Teaching Legal Drafting Effectively and Efficiently – By Dispensing with the Myths. 57 *Journal of Legal Education* (2007) pp. 448-466.

Wolff, Chinese Outbound Investments in the Food Sector: Hungry for Much More!. 69 (3) *Food and Drug Law Journal* (2014) pp. 399-428.

Wolff, Pathological Foreign Investment Projects in China: Patchwork or Trendsetting of the Supreme People's Court?. 44 (3) *The International Lawyer* (Fall 2010) pp. 1001-1018.

Wolff, PRC Company Law: One Country, Many Systems?. 3 *Hong Kong Lawyer* (2001) pp. 37-42.

Wolski, Bobette, Why, How and What to Practice: Integrating Skills Teaching and Learning in the Undergraduate Curriculum. 52 *Journal of Legal Education* (2002) pp. 287-302.

Books

Alias, Nor Aziah, 'Incorporating Cultural Components into the Design of an Affective Support Tool for the Malaysian Online Distance Learners' in Edmundson, Andrea (ed) *Cases on Globalized and Culturally appropriate e-learning.* Pennsylvania, IGI Global 2011.

Atlas, Joel et al., *A Guide to Teaching Lawyering Skills Durham.* North Carolina: Carolina Academia Press, (2012).

Bligh, Donald A., 'The Lecture Method Alone is Rarely Adequate' in *What's the Use of Lectures.* (1st ed) San Francisco, Jossey-Bass (2000) pp. 223-230.

Bonk, Curtis J. et al., 'Future Directions of Blended Learning in Higher Education and Workplace Learning Settings' in Bonk, Curtis J. & Graham, Charles R. (ed) *The Handbook of Blended Learning: global perspectives, local designs.* (1st ed) San Francisco, Pfeiffer (2006) pp. 550-565.

Exley, Kate & Dennick, Reg, 'Why Lecture?' in *Giving a Lecture: From Presenting to Teaching.* (2nd ed) NewYork, Routledge (2009) pp. 1-13.

Graham, Charles R., 'Blended learning systems' in Bonk, Curtis J. and Graham, Charles R. (ed) *The Handbook of Blended Learning: global perspectives, local designs.* (1st ed) San Francisco, Pfeiffer (2006) pp. 3-21.

Hativa, Nira, 'Lecturing and Explaining' and 'Active Learning During Lectures' in *Teaching for Effective Learning in Higher Education.* Boston, Kluwer Academic Publishers (2000) 71-110.

Henderson, George & Nash, Susan Smith, 'Lectures' in *Excellence in College Teaching and Learning.* Illinois, Charles C Tomas Publisher, Ltd. (2007) pp. 25-43.

Knowles, Malcolm, 'Andragogy: An emerging technology for adult learning' in Edwards, Richard, Hanson, Ann and Raggatt, Peter (ed) *Boundaries of Adult Learning.* (1st ed) Abingdon England, New York, Routledge (1996) pp. 82-98.

Le Brun, Marlene & Johnstone, Richard, *The Quiet Revolution: Improving Student Learning in Law.* Australia, The Law Book Company Limited (1994).

Light, Grey et al., 'Lecturing: large-group teaching' in *Learning and Teaching in Higher Education: The Reflective Professional.* (2nd ed) London, SAGE Publications Ltd. (2009) pp. 105-126.

MacDonald, Janet, 'Blended Learning and Pragmatism' in *Blended Learning and Online Tutoring: planning learner support and activity design.* (2nd ed) Aldershot; Burlington, VT: Gower (2008) pp. 31-44.

McLeish, John, *The Lecture Method* The Great Britain, Heffers of Cambridge (1968).

McNeely, Ben, 'Using Technology as a Learning Tool, Not Just the Cool Next Thing' in Oblinger, Diana G. (Author) & Oblinger, James L. (Contributor) *Educating the Net Generation.* Educause (2005) pp. 4.1-4.10.

The Carnegie Report - Sullivan, William M. et al., The Carnegie Foundation for the Advancement of Teaching, *Educating Lawyers: preparation for the profession of law.* San Francisco, Jossey-Bass/Wiley (2007).

Thornton, Margaret, 'Jettisoning the Critical' in *Privatising the Public University: The Case of Law.* Abingdon, Oxon; New York, Routledge a GlassHouse book (2012) pp. 59-100.

Webb, Julian et al., *Lawyer's Skills.* Oxford: Oxford University Press (2011).

Wiley, David & Green, Cable, 'Why Openness in Education?' in Oblinger, Diana (ed) *Game Changers.* EDUCAUSE Publications (2012).

Wolff, Lutz-Christian, *Mergers & Acquisitions in China: Law and Practice.* (4th ed./5th ed.) Hong Kong: CCH Hong Kong Limited. (2010/2015).

Wolff, Lutz-Christian, *The Law of Cross-border Business Transactions – Principles, Concepts, Skills.* Alphen aan den Rijn: Kluwer Law International (2013).

Others

Audacity, Audacity 2.1.1 Manual. (11 July 2015), http://manual.audacityteam.org/o/

Forret, Peter, Video filesize calculator (2006-2015), http://toolstud.io/video/filesize.php?

Potts, J.P., A new model for open sharing April 20, MIT Open Courseware, Massachusetts Institute of Technology (2005), http://ocw.mit.edu/courses/special-programs/sp-772-internet-technology-in-local-and-global-communities-spring-2005-summer-2005/lecture-notes/l11_opencoursewa.pdf (visited on 30 August 2014, but no longer available online in the original form).

Wood, Mary, FLIPPED: Prof Models New Way of Teaching, UVA LAW (Fall 2012). http://www.law.virginia.edu/html/alumni/uvalawyer/fi2/flipped.htm.Yeh, Benson, 'How to flip the class-room well – BTS Flipping' .Seminar at the Chinese University of Hong Kong on 24 October 2014.

Woodford, Chris, Streaming media (3 November 2014), http://www.explainthatstuff.com/streamingmedia.html

MIX
Papier aus verantwortungsvollen Quellen
Paper from responsible sources
FSC® C105338

If you have any concerns about our products,
you can contact us on
ProductSafety@springernature.com

In case Publisher is established outside the EU,
the EU authorized representative is:
Springer Nature Customer Service Center GmbH
Europaplatz 3, 69115 Heidelberg, Germany

Printed by Libri Plureos GmbH
in Hamburg, Germany